How to Fight
Heart Disease & Win

How to Fight Heart Disease & Win
Published by Agora Health Books
Alice Wessendorf, Managing Editor
Ken Danz, Copy Editor

Additional orders and inquiries can be directed to Agora Health Books,
Customer Service Department, 819 N. Charles Street, Baltimore, MD
21201.

ISBN 1-891434-11-X
Printed in the United States of America

AGORA HEALTH BOOKS
819 N. Charles St.
Baltimore, MD 21201

HOW TO FIGHT
HEART DISEASE & WIN

WILLIAM L. FISCHER

AGORA HEALTH BOOKS
BALTIMORE, MARYLAND

DISCLAIMER

All material in this publication is provided for information only and may not be construed as medical advice or instruction. No action should be taken based solely on the contents of this publication; instead, readers should consult appropriate health professionals on any matter relating to their health and well-being.

The information and opinions provided in this publication are believed to be accurate and sound, based on the best judgment available to the authors, but readers who fail to consult with appropriate health authorities assume the risk of any injuries. The publisher is not responsible for errors or omissions.

THE INFORMATION PRESENTED HERE HAS NOT BEEN EVALUATED BY THE U.S. FOOD & DRUG ADMINISTRATION. THIS PRODUCT IS NOT INTENDED TO DIAGNOSE, TREAT, CURE, OR PREVENT ANY DISEASE.

TABLE OF CONTENTS

• C H A P T E R 1 •

Heart Disease: From the Inside Out

If we've heard it once, we've heard it a thousand times: Heart-related disease is the No. 1 killer in the United States. This has been the case since 1900, according to the American Heart Association (AHA)—a leading authority on heart and vascular diseases. Since 1940, the number of deaths from heart disease has increased, due, at least in part, to the aging of the U.S. population.

An epidemic of heart disease began to develop in the 1930s. In the 1940s, the U.S. Public Health Service (PHS) decided it was time to undertake a large-scale study to investigate why it had become rampant. PHS officials wanted to know how people who developed heart disease differed from those who escaped it.

In 1948, the National Heart Institute (now known as the National Heart, Lung, and Blood Institute [NHLBI]) embarked on an ambitious project it named the Framingham Heart Study. At the time, little was known about the general causes of heart disease and stroke. The objective of the Framingham Heart Study (FHS) was to identify the common factors or characteristics that contribute to these conditions. FHS researchers planned to watch, over a long time period, a large group of participants who had no overt symptoms or heart disease and had not yet experienced a heart attack or stroke.

The researchers recruited 5,209 men and women between the ages of 30 and 62 from the town of Framingham, Massachusetts, and began the first round of extensive physical examinations and lifestyle interviews that they would later analyze for common patterns. The subjects returned to the laboratory every two years for detailed medical histories, physical exams, and laboratory tests.

In 1971, the study enrolled a second-generation group. More than 5,000 of the original participants' adult children and their spouses participated in similar exams. Other offshoots of the original studies have been, and continue to be, conducted by FHS researchers. Over the years, careful monitoring of all participants has contributed to a wide range of valuable information about heart-related disease.

Many, many other researchers and groups have joined the fight against heart disease since the initiation of the FHS. Some operate within the realm of "modern" medicine while others focus on "alternative" or "complementary" methods of prevention. Across the board, there is now convincing scientific evidence to show that our lifestyle choices, including our diet and exercise habits, can significantly increase our risk of developing heart disease. The evidence is equally significant that we can make different choices to reduce and even prevent its occurrence.

That's what this book, *How to Fight Heart Disease & Win*, is all about. It's for people who want to know the facts about heart disease and then take the steps needed for better heart health. This path begins from the inside of our bodies and has many different side streets.

- What is heart disease?

- How does our cardiovascular (CV) system work?

- What can go wrong?

- What are the risk factors?

- What is the role of "modern" medicine?

- Just how important are diet, vitamin and herbal supplements, and exercise to prevention?

What is Heart Disease?

Although the illness in question is commonly referred to as "heart disease," the official, and more comprehensive, term is *cardiovascular disease (CVD)*. This includes any disorder that affects the heart or blood vessels. In fact, CVD can take a number of forms, many of them overlapping, as you'll see. The term "cardiovascular" also lets us know that, although the heart certainly is the most valuable player in our body, it depends on the blood vessels and the lungs to work.

According to the *2001 Heart and Stroke Statistical Update* published by the American Heart Association, CVD occurs in many forms. The most current statistics list the following as being the most prevalent heart-related conditions in the United States: high blood pressure, coronary heart disease (CHD), stroke, congenital cardiovascular defects, and congestive heart failure (CHF).

More than 61 million Americans have one or more of these conditions. One in five has some form of CVD. Looking at the numbers gives us a good idea just how many of us are affected by CVD.

- 50 million of us have **high blood pressure.**

- 12,400,000 have **coronary heart disease**, which

5

includes myocardial infarctions (heart attacks) and angina (chest pain).

- 4,700,000 suffer from **congestive heart failure**.

- 4,500,000 have had **strokes**.

In reaction to the association's statistical update, Dr. David Faxon, AHA president, said that the "most surprising finding is that heart-disease and stroke numbers are not going down." "For many years," he added, "they did, but now we are seeing a leveling off, and, in fact, we are seeing an increase in some groups, such as African-American women." He cites the reasons for the leveling off as the aging of the population and the "growing problems" of diabetes and obesity, both of which greatly contribute to the increase in heart disease.

Of *all* the deaths each year in the United States, cardiovascular diseases cause more than 40 percent. Almost half of the people who died this year had coronary heart disease specifically. Stroke isn't far behind. High blood pressure, congestive heart failure, and atherosclerosis are also contributing factors.

Many of the individuals who died from cardiovascular diseases were under the age of 65, and 52 percent were women—with men following close behind at 46.9 percent. More than half of those deaths occur suddenly, as a result of cardiac arrest. A high percentage of the people who died didn't have a clue (no prior symptoms) that they even had heart disease.

Caring for people with cardiovascular disease currently costs billions of dollars, and the rise in health-care costs assures us that it will get more expensive. Costs were estimated to be over $298 billion for 2001, and they are expected to rise to over $329 billion in 2002. Most of the cost is for inpatient hospitalization, so, as AHA's

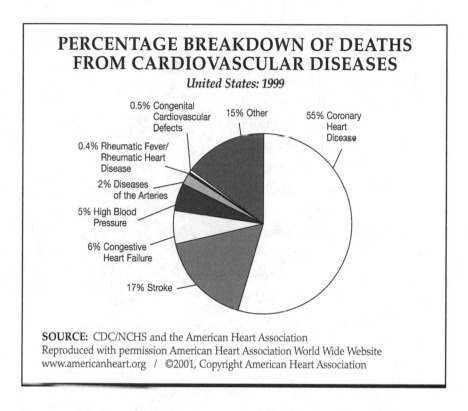

PERCENTAGE BREAKDOWN OF DEATHS FROM CARDIOVASCULAR DISEASES
United States: 1999

0.5% Congenital Cardiovascular Defects

15% Other

55% Coronary Heart Disease

0.4% Rheumatic Fever/ Rheumatic Heart Disease

2% Diseases of the Arteries

5% High Blood Pressure

6% Congestive Heart Failure

17% Stroke

SOURCE: CDC/NCHS and the American Heart Association
Reproduced with permission American Heart Association World Wide Website
www.americanheart.org / ©2001, Copyright American Heart Association

Faxon said, "anything that prevents the disease and complications and the need for rehospitalization" can reduce the cost.

"For instance, taking a beta-blocker, an ACE inhibitor, or statin drug after a heart attack dramatically reduces the chance of another heart attack or death," he said. The AHA also believes that lifestyle changes have the greatest effect on preventing death and illnesses associated with cardiovascular disease.

"While we have made modest effects in regard to smoking and cholesterol awareness, we are losing ground in high-blood-pressure awareness," Faxon said. "Both men and women need to stop smoking, eat right, and exercise and know their blood pressure and cholesterol readings and keep them at target levels," he advised.

How Does Our CV System Work?

The cornerstone of the cardiovascular system is, of course, the heart—a hollow but thick muscle that pumps blood throughout the body by coordinated nerve impulses and muscular contractions. An average adult heart, which is about the size of a clenched fist, weighs between 7 and 15 ounces, depending on the individual. It's centrally located between the lungs, although most of it lies to the left of the breastbone.

The heart muscle consists of three layers, but the central layer, called the *myocardium,* forms the bulk of the heart wall. The heart also consists of four chambers: two ventricles (left and right) and two atria (left and right). The ventricles take up more space in the heart, and do more work, than the atria.

The cardiac cycle begins when the *sinoatrial (SA) node* (a cluster of cells in the

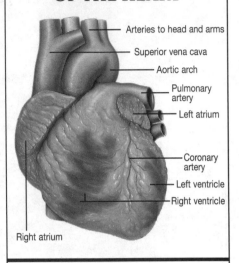

EXTERIOR STRUCTURES OF THE HEART

- Arteries to head and arms
- Superior vena cava
- Aortic arch
- Pulmonary artery
- Left atrium
- Coronary artery
- Left ventricle
- Right ventricle
- Right atrium

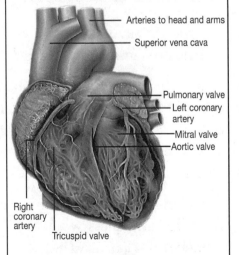

INTERIOR STRUCTURES OF THE HEART

- Arteries to head and arms
- Superior vena cava
- Pulmonary valve
- Left coronary artery
- Mitral valve
- Aortic valve
- Right coronary artery
- Tricuspid valve

Used with the permission of Yale-New Haven Hospital, New Haven, CT.

Medical illustration by Patrick Lynch, Yale School of Medicine. The copyright holder reserves all rights.

heart muscle) in the right atrium generates an electrical impulse that makes the heart chambers contract. This node (one of many in the heart) includes specialized "pacemaker cells" with a rhythm that is independent of any other nerve impulses in the body. As you'll read in Chapter 3, the body's natural pacemaker may break down, and if this happens, an artificial pacemaker may be inserted into the body.

The SA node normally fires about 70 to 75 beats per minute, although certain activities, such as physical exercise, may cause it to fire faster. If the node fails to generate an impulse, the role of pacemaker shifts to another component of the heart. In essence, it is the SA node that determines our *pulse* and the pulse that sets the rhythm of the entire system.

At each heartbeat (or contraction), the left ventricle (the heart's main pumping chamber) receives blood full of oxygen and nutrients from the left atrium and sends it to the *aorta* (the body's largest artery). From the aorta, the blood goes into smaller vessels and on to all organs and tissues of the body. The heart also receives its blood supply from this cycle via the *coronary arteries*, which branch out from the aorta.

The "used" blood (blood with no oxygen and nutrients) returns to the heart through the right atrium and then goes into the right ventricle, which forces the blood to the lungs to be replenished. The lungs remove the carbon dioxide from the blood and inject fresh oxygen, and the cardiac cycle begins again.

As the above description shows, the vascular system has two enormous responsibilities.

■ It transports oxygen and nutrients around the circulatory system and into all parts of the body.

- It returns the deoxygenated blood from the body to the lungs, which remove the waste products and supply new oxygen for the next cycle.

When any part of this process malfunctions, our hearts, and our lives, are in jeopardy. As you'll find out in Chapter 2, many of these "malfunctions" can be traced back to blood flow—or, actually, lack of proper blood flow.

What Can Go Wrong?

Our cardiovascular system does a lot of work, doesn't it? It truly does live up to its reputation as amazing. Consider these interesting facts.

- With each heartbeat, the bloodstream transports oxygen and nutrients to the approximately 300 trillion cells in the body.
- A heart "at rest" pumps 1 million barrels of blood in an average lifetime. That's enough to fill 3.3 supertankers. (Imagine the amount of blood that it pumps during exercise or times of stress, when it's working harder!)
- In 50 years, the energy expended by the heart is enough to lift a battleship out of the water.

Not surprisingly, this valuable engine can break down.

Consider, for example, coronary heart disease, which begins when *plaque* (which consists of cholesterol and other fats or lipids, calcium, and a blood-clotting material called fibrin) builds up and, eventually, narrows or clogs the coronary arteries. This condition, known as *atherosclerosis* (or hardening of the arteries), occurs progressively over a period of time.

When too much plaque collects in the arteries, the blood flow slows; as a result, the heart doesn't receive the oxygen and nutrients it needs. As explained thoroughly in the next chapter, this sometimes leads to chest pain—or *angina*. If a coronary artery gets blocked completely, the result is a ***heart attack***.

In the above example, it is the *overabundance* of plaque in the arteries that is at the root of "what went wrong." In the case of cardiovascular disease, plaque is clearly the heart's most powerful enemy. In the next chapter, I will explain in more detail how plaque and atherosclerosis lead to cardiovascular disease.

What are the Risk Factors?

Researchers with the Framingham Heart Study gave the world the term ***risk factor*** to describe conditions or modes of behavior that increase the chance of developing a disease. They discovered that although several factors are beyond our control, there are many that we can modify, treat, or control to lower our risk of developing diseases, including those of the cardiovascular system.

In addition to separating risk factors into those that are *uncontrollable* and those that are *controllable*, researchers further divide them into those that are major and those that are contributing. ***Major risk factors*** are those that have been proven to increase the risk of heart disease. ***Contributing risk factors*** are those that are important but, as the American Heart Association clarifies, are somewhat ambiguous in that their "significance and prevalence haven't yet been precisely determined."

Some risk factors can be changed, treated, or modified, and some cannot. If you have more than one risk factor, your chance of developing heart disease increases. And if you have many risk factors, your chances of developing heart disease increase even more.

Controlling as many risk factors as you can through lifestyle changes, vitamin and herbal supplements, and, if needed, prescription drugs should help reduce your risk of heart disease.

Major Uncontrollable Risk Factors

In the case of disease, there are indeed some things you just can't control. In the case of coronary heart disease (CHD) and stroke, the following are the *major uncontrollable risk factors*. Although the risk factors for the two problems are very similar, you'll see below that researchers do make some distinctions.

Increasing age. As we age, our hearts tend to get sluggish. Four out of five people who die of CHD are age 65 or older. The chance of having a stroke more than doubles for each decade of life after age 55. While stroke is common among the elderly, 28 percent of people under 65 also have strokes.

Gender. Men may have an earlier risk of heart attacks than women do; after menopause, however, the risk increases for women. This is because women are somewhat protected from heart disease until menopause because they are producing estrogen. Beginning at age 65 and older, everyone seems to have the same risk. Interestingly, statistics show that women who have heart attacks are more likely than men to die from them within a few weeks. Some heart experts believe this is the case because women are more surprised than men that they are having a heart attack and get help less quickly.

In the case of stroke, the latest data show that the overall morbidity (in terms of both incidence and prevalence) is about equal for men and women. However, women account for more than half of the total deaths from stroke.

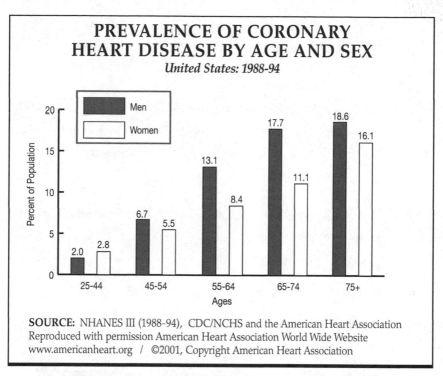

PREVALENCE OF CORONARY HEART DISEASE BY AGE AND SEX
United States: 1988-94

SOURCE: NHANES III (1988-94), CDC/NCHS and the American Heart Association
Reproduced with permission American Heart Association World Wide Website
www.americanheart.org / ©2001, Copyright American Heart Association

Heredity, family history, and race. Framingham Heart Study researchers believe that a family history of early heart disease—say, a father or brother having been diagnosed before 55 or a mother or sister having been diagnosed before 65—or stroke is particularly predictive of trouble. In other words, children of parents with CVD are more likely to develop it themselves. Risk factors (including high blood pressure, diabetes, and obesity) may also be passed from one generation to another.

Researchers have found that some forms of cardiovascular disease are more common among certain racial and ethnic groups. For example, studies have shown that black Americans have more severe high blood pressure, and a greater risk of heart disease and stroke, than whites do. Risk factors for cardiovascular disease in other racial and ethnic groups (Mexican-Americans, American Indians, native Hawaiians, and Asian-Americans) are being studied.

Major but Controllable Risk Factors

With only slight variations among research groups, the following are generally considered to be the major controllable factors of CVD. The first three are clearly the leaders of the pack.

- High blood pressure
- High blood-cholesterol and triglyceride levels
- Smoking
- Obesity
- Physical inactivity
- Diabetes
- Stress

High blood pressure. I cannot emphasize enough the importance of understanding this cardiovascular disease, which is also called hypertension. I discuss it in detail in Chapter 2, and you'll find many references to it throughout the book. Here's a review of why it's so important to keep blood pressure within normal ranges.

High blood pressure forces the heart to work harder, which causes it to become larger and weaker over time. It also increases the risks of a stroke, a heart attack, congestive heart failure, and kidney failure. When high blood pressure exists along with obesity, smoking, high blood-cholesterol levels, or diabetes, the risk of a heart attack or stroke increases several times.

High blood-cholesterol and triglyceride levels. The chance that we will get coronary heart disease increases when our blood-cholesterol and triglyceride levels are high. When we have other risk factors (such as high blood pressure), the chance of developing it rises even further. Although lipid levels are affected by many uncontrollable factors, such as age, gender, and heredity, we can often control them through dietary intervention and increased exercise. In fact, according to the American Heart Association, just a 10-percent decrease in cholesterol levels may result in an estimated 30 percent reduction in the incidence of coronary heart disease.

Unfortunately, many of us choose not to make a commitment to a better diet and more exercise and must advance to the next step of treatment, which is one of the cholesterol-lowering medications that will be discussed in Chapter 3. You'll learn more about cholesterol, triglycerides, and other fatty substances in Chapter 2.

Smoking. In the past, smoking was usually connected to an increased risk of lung cancer; it may surprise you, however, to find out that it also increases the risks of heart disease and peripheral vascular disease (disease in the vessels that supply blood to the arms and legs). More than 400,000 Americans die each year of smoking-related illnesses, and many of these deaths can be traced back to the effect that smoking has had on the heart and blood vessels.

For starters, smoking increases the heart rate, tightens major arteries, and increases the chance of irregular heartbeats. All of these factors make the heart work harder. Smoking also raises blood pressure, which increases the risk of stroke in people who already have heart problems. (See Chapter 2 for more on smoking.)

Obesity. Weighing even slightly more than ideal for your height increases your risk for heart disease. More than 106.9 million U.S. adults (20 and older) are considered overweight, and 43.6 million are considered obese.

The more pounds over your ideal weight you are, the greater the risk factor. Exceeding your *ideal* weight by 30 percent puts a real strain on your heart and raises your blood pressure. People with too many extra pounds have higher levels of LDL cholesterol and triglycerides in their blood and lower levels of high-density lipoprotein (HDL), which is one of the "good" guys, as you'll read in Chapter 2. Diabetes also is more likely to develop in overweight people.

Where the weight is accumulated is also of extreme importance for both sexes. People who are apple-shaped (gain fat around the middle) are at a much higher risk than those who are pear-shaped (gain fat around the hips). Those who have excess body fat, particularly around the waist, are more likely to develop

---

CALCULATE YOUR BODY-MASS INDEX (BMI)

Your body-mass index compares your height to your weight to determine obesity. A BMI of 19 to 24.9 is considered normal, a BMI of 25 to 29.9 indicates you are overweight, and a reading of over 30 indicates obesity. To calculate your own BMI, multiply your weight in pounds by 704.5, then multiply your height in inches by your height in inches, and then divide your first result by your second result. The number you get is your BMI. Below is an example:

If your height is 5 feet 10 inches and you weigh 140 pounds
140 x 704.5 = 98,630
70 x 70 = 4,900
98,630 divided by 4,900 = 20.1

If you are looking for a simpler method for figuring out your BMI, look on-line. There are many automatic BMI calculators to choose from.

heart disease and stroke—even when they have no other risk factors.

Many obese and otherwise overweight people have difficulty losing weight. But experts say that losing as little as 10 or 20 pounds can help lower one's heart-disease risk. Although some individuals may need professional help to lose weight, others can do so by eating less and exercising more. (See Chapters 4 and 6 for more on the importance of diet and exercise.)

Physical inactivity. Only about 22 percent of American adults report regular sustained physical activity of any intensity (activity lasting 30 minutes or more) five times a week. At 55 and over, about 38 percent of us admit to sedentary lifestyles. People who do not exercise have a 30 percent to 50 percent greater risk of developing high blood pressure and a greater risk of having a heart attack than people who do exercise.

As Chapter 6 explains, experts recommend a moderate-to-vigorous level of physical activity but say even a lower level of exercise may be beneficial if it occurs regularly. As you'll see, there are numerous benefits associated with exercise—and it can be fun!

Diabetes. Having diabetes increases a person's overall risk of cardiovascular disease. People who are afflicted with it often have high cholesterol levels and are overweight. The AHA estimates that 65 percent of patients with diabetes die of some form of cardiovascular disease.

In 1999, the association added diabetes to its official list of risk factors for coronary heart disease and stroke. The National Heart, Lung and Blood Institute (NHLBI) has ini-

tiated a large clinical trial to study high blood-sugar, cholesterol, and hypertension levels, all possible symptoms of
diabetes and risk factors for heart disease.

In May 2001, the NHLBI's National Cholesterol
Education Program (NCEP) released new cholesterol
guidelines that upgraded diabetes to a *primary* risk factor
for heart disease. (It was formerly classified as "one of the
many factors".) Research has shown that diabetes is as significant as coronary artery disease when it comes to a 10-
year risk of developing heart problems. The NCEP recommends that patients with diabetes follow the same guidelines as those diagnosed with coronary heart disease.

Those who know they have diabetes are no doubt
already under a doctor's care, and control of blood-sugar
levels can reduce the risk of heart disease. Unfortunately,
the symptoms of diabetes often go unnoticed. If the disease
is untreated, it can cause serious damage to the heart, eyes,
kidneys, and nerves. It also has a tendency to mask the
symptoms of heart disease.

Like high blood cholesterol, high blood pressure, and
excessive weight, diabetes can be controlled, and even pre-
vented, by a diet low in fat, salt, and cholesterol; by regular exercise; and if necessary by medication.

Stress. The term "stress" really needs no introduction. We
all know what stress is. We feel it every day. Put simply,
stress is the end result of conflict between the demands of
life and our ability to meet those demands. What causes us
stress, and how we react to that stress, is as individual as
we are. The most common stressors are family, work, and
finances. At one time or another, we have all let stress influ-

ence our health behaviors.

For example, people under stress may overeat, start smoking, or smoke more than they otherwise would. Not surprisingly, researchers have found a relationship between the level of stress in a person's life and coronary heart disease. It's easy to see why stress is considered a contributing risk factor for heart disease, although little is known about its effects.

Researchers, at this time, are not saying that stress causes heart disease, but they do believe that in the very least it aggravates heart conditions and that people are more likely to have heart attacks during stressful times. The Texas Heart Institute (THI) in Houston provides several examples.

- When we are under stress, our hearts race and our blood pressure rises—increasing the demand for oxygen. When a person's heart is diseased, it can't pump blood fast enough to supply the oxygen needed, and, unfortunately, the result may be angina or chest pain.

- During stressful times, the nervous system releases extra hormones (such as adrenaline). These hormones raise one's blood pressure, which can injure the lining of the arteries. When the arteries heal, the walls may harden or thicken—making it easier for plaque to build up.

- Blood clots are more likely to form during times of stress and could block an artery already narrowed by plaque. This may lead to a heart attack.

Here's what Dr. Denton Cooley, president, surgeon-in-chief, and founder of THI, has to say on the subject.

"Managing stress can improve your life, no matter how healthy you are." But in order to do this, you must be able to identify when you are feeling overwhelmed. Common symptoms include a racing heart, sudden sweating, sudden anger, an upset stomach, headaches, anxiety, tensing of muscles, and binge eating and drinking, to name a few.

"Once you recognize that you are under stress, try to pinpoint the cause of it," Cooley recommends. In order to find your personal pattern of stress, write down when you feel that way. Think about ways you could avoid such situations. As Cooley says, "You cannot change all the situations that cause you stress, but you can change your response to those situations. There are a number ways to reduce the effects of stress on your mind and body. Exercising, crying, taking warm baths, and breathing deeply are just a few ways to minimize stress. Find a method that works for you." (See Chapter 6 for more ideas.)

Other Contributing Factors

Although the factors discussed above are the most-researched and most-proven risk factors of cardiovascular disease, there are other important ones (listed below) that will be discussed in more detail later in this book.

Excessive alcohol intake. Drinking more than a moderate amount of alcohol can lead to heart-related problems like high blood pressure, strokes, an irregular heartbeat, and cardiomyopathy (disease of the heart muscle). The average drink has between 100 and 200 calories, which will often add fat to the body. As I already mentioned, excess weight is one of the major risk factors of heart disease.

Sex hormones. As the levels of the female hormone estrogen decline in a woman's body, her risk of heart disease rises. Studies have shown that estrogen helps protect women against heart attacks by raising levels of high-density lipoprotein (HDL), or "good cholesterol," in the blood.

Birth-control pills. The risk of developing blood clots and having a heart attack rises for women who take "the pill" (particularly for those who also smoke).

Emerging Risk Factors

And if the above weren't enough to scare anyone into taking heart health more seriously, there's even a category frequently called *emerging risk factors.* Researchers are still gathering scientific data about these factors, but they're confident that they play an important role in heart disease.

- homocysteine (an amino acid found in our bodies)
- infections and inflammation
- apolipoprotein (a type of lipoprotein)

Homocysteine. Research indicates that high blood levels of this amino acid may contribute to the build-up of plaque in the arteries. Homocysteine does this by promoting the growth of smooth muscle cells just below an artery's inner wall. These cells multiply rapidly and create a bulge that protrudes into the artery. Such bulges become traps for the cholesterol, blood byproducts, and calcium that create the plaque.

Framingham Heart Study researchers say that homocysteine also causes blood platelets to stick together and form clots. Furthermore, it makes blood vessels less flexible. This means that it's harder for the vessels to widen so that blood can flow freely. Although high blood levels of homocysteine relate partly to genetics, a better diet and more exercise may help decrease them.

Although Framingham researchers believe this is how homocysteine causes problems for the heart, other researchers are more cautious. The AHA, for example, agrees that there is some evidence that high levels of homocysteine may have an effect on atherosclerosis by damaging the inner lining of arteries and promoting blood clots but cautions that no *direct* link has been established.

Other researchers also point out that no one has proven yet that lowering the levels will definitely help prevent heart-related diseases. However, lowering homocysteine levels is generally considered safe, and since it may have some positive results, many experts recommend trying to do so. As you'll see in Chapter 5, there are a number of vitamin and herbal supplements that researchers have found to safely lower homocysteine in the blood.

Infections and inflammation. For several years now, researchers have also been studying the link between inflammation (caused by infection) and atherosclerosis. When the immune system is fighting an infection, the body releases large amounts of a substance called *C-reactive protein*—which is being studied as a marker of blood-vessel inflammation.

Researchers at Johannes Gutenberg University in Mainz, Germany, recently published the findings of a three-year study on this subject. They found a "significant association" between the number of viral and bacterial infections a person has been exposed to and the level of atherosclerosis. Specifically, people with more infections were more likely to have heart disease and were more likely to die from it than those with fewer infections.

The AHA gets even more specific about this likelihood. It says that men with the highest levels of C-reactive protein in their blood have three times the chance of a heart attack and two times the chance of a stroke than men with lower levels.

In spite of these findings and opinions, though, some scientists continue to question whether common infections (such as the flu, herpes, and pneumonia) cause heart disease or whether some other mechanism is involved. Dr. Paul Ridker, director of the Center for Cardiovascular Disease Prevention at Brigham and Women's Hospital and a professor at the Harvard School of Medicine in Boston cautioned against mistaking an association. "It doesn't mean that everyone who gets an infection will develop heart attacks and strokes," he said.

Coming from a slightly different angle, the benefit of preventive aspirin therapy was greatest among individuals with the highest levels of underlying inflammation. As discussed in Chapter 3, aspirin is both an anti-inflammatory and a blood-thinning agent. This suggests that other anti-inflammatory therapies also might help prevent heart disease.

Apolipoproteins. As described thoroughly in Chapter 2, low-density-lipoprotein (LDL) molecules carry most of the disease-promoting cholesterol throughout the bloodstream. But there are similar molecules, called *apolipoproteins,* that some researchers believe might be a risk factor for early heart disease. There are two types: apoA-1 and apoB. You might see these identified also as Lp(a) and

Lp(b). Although apoA-1 is thought to carry cholesterol in the blood, the specific roles of each are still being debated.

Framingham Heart Study researchers, for example, say that Lp(a) appears to promote plaque in the arteries by preventing the breakup of clots. Another study found that levels of apoB and the ratio of apoB to apoA-1 were strongly related to the risk of suffering a fatal heart attack. These researchers believe that apoliprotein tests have a "little better predictive power" than HDL and LDL cholesterol tests. However, since the methods of performing them are not yet standardized, these tests are not commonly used.

Metabolic syndrome X. The May 2001 National Cholesterol Education Program guidelines state that patients and physicians should become aware of *metabolic syndrome X*— a cluster of specific risk factors. People with this cluster have four to 20 times more chance of having a heart attack than those who don't have it. Here are the factors that metabolic syndrome X includes.

- elevated insulin levels (insulin resistance)
- central obesity (around the middle)
- high levels of both LDL cholesterol and triglycerides
- hypertension (high blood pressure)
- Type II diabetes

The first factor listed—insulin resistance—is of particular interest, because it is considered a key contributor to metabolic syndrome X. This condition causes the pancreas to secrete an excessive amount of insulin, which circulates unused in the blood but stimulates a craving for more food. The AHA estimates that up to 30 percent of the adult population has insulin resistance. Obesity and lack of physical activity are key contributors to the development of this syndrome.

Modern Medicine and the Heart

As we already know, modern medicine does not take a one-size-fits-all approach. What helps one person may not help another, and it seems that the practitioners of modern medicine experiment with different treatment options until one, they hope, works. Findings from statistical studies do, of course, better the odds of success, but there is simply no guarantee about how, or even if, the body will react positively.

For health-care consumers, this can be frustrating and disappointing—particularly for those who rely totally on their physicians to solve their health problems. Consider a person who has heart disease, for example.

Most doctors urge their patients to lose weight, improve their eating habits, and start exercising, but they cannot *make* their patients do anything unless they're willing. Eventually, those unhealthy habits lead to unmistakable signs that's "something wrong." At that point, they go to the doctor's office for help.

Once there, they undergo some tests. If the tests show certain results, the doctor treats them. Often, "treatment" means giving them one or more prescriptions for medication. "Give me a pill and make it go away" is a common desire. Sometimes the pills work, and sometimes they don't. When they don't, the patients undergo more tests—usually more complicated than the first ones. Often, these show that they need surgery or a similar type of invasive intervention.

What we call modern medicine is treatment for the damage that's already been done. As you'll see in Chapter 3, the offerings available to repair the damage are many—as are the accompanying risks. This chapter only begins to list the options for diagnostic tests and drug therapies available for heart disease. It also touches upon a few of the most common operations available for fixing heart-related problems that can't be fixed by drugs.

But, in reality, modern medicine is a real team effort. It's up to us to go beyond what our physicians tell us. It's a rare medical doctor who suggests we consider therapeutic doses of vitamins or herbs as aids or cures. It's up to us to educate ourselves about natural alternatives.

As Dr. Denton Cooley says, "Many people take better care of their cars than their bodies. They are careful to change the oil, have regular tune-ups, and use the proper gasoline. When it comes to their bodies, however, they fuel them with high-fat and high-salt meals, smoke, and don't exercise routinely. Medical advances can't eradicate heart disease. Good health depends largely on people taking positive action."

Prevention Involves Us

As the National Heart, Lung, and Blood Institute puts it, "Changing one's habits remains the most effective way to stop the disease from progressing." We all know that changing our habits, particularly those involving food and exercise, is no easy task. Lucky for us all, however, proper diet and exercise are considered the first lines of defense against heart disease, and there is an abundance of information that we can use to modify our behaviors and get back on the heart-healthy track.

The good news is that we can take steps to reduce our risks of developing heart disease. There's even an official term for this. It's called *therapeutic lifestyle change* (TLC): a cholesterol-lowering diet, supplements of vitamins and herbs, physical activity, and weight management. TLC is for anyone who's at risk for heart disease.

Because cardiovascular diseases usually develop over a long period of time, we have opportunities throughout our lives to prevent or control them. Preventive care can begin early or late, but the research is clear that it does at least slow the development of cardiovascular disease.

As this book will show, a healthier heart is within your reach. Those who are willing to take positive action, such as making needed lifestyle changes, can fight heart disease and win!

CHAPTER 2

Cardiovascular Disease in Depth

Over the last 50 or more years, scientists from all over the world have studied the cardiovascular system. They know how it works and why it stops working. Physicians know how to diagnose most heart conditions, and proponents of both modern and alternative medicine know how to prevent, treat and, in some cases, even reverse it.

The AHA statistics cited in Chapter 1 tell us a lot about our bodies when they are in a dying state. These statistics and others remove every shadow of a doubt that cardiovascular disease (CVD) is killing too many of us. Luckily, there also is no scientific doubt that determining our risk factors and taking steps to lower their control over our health can help us live longer, healthier lives.

To return to the AHA's statistics, approximately 50 million Americans have high blood pressure (hypertension). This is the most prevalent heart-related condition in the United States and also a symptom of coronary heart disease (CHD). More than 12 million Americans suffer have some form of CHD, which also includes *arrhythmia*, *angina*, and *heart attacks*. Other heart-related conditions include congestive heart failure (CHF), strokes, carotid artery disease, and peripheral vascular disease.

Although each type of CVD is unique, all have at least one symptom in common: **athcrosclerosis** (more commonly known as hardening of the arteries). This condition contributes to about 75 percent of the deaths resulting from CVD, according to the Framingham Heart Study. Knowing how it develops is a good starting point for understanding how to prevent it—and the other diseases to which it leads.

Atherosclerosis

When associated with atherosclerosis, the term "hardening" refers to a condition in which the arteries become narrow and stiff and blood flow to and from the heart is blocked. The symptoms of this slow, progressive condition may start as early as childhood or as late as middle age.

As stated in the first chapter, atherosclerosis is characterized by the build-up of yellowish **plaque** in the **lumen** (the narrow, inner opening in the arteries through which blood flows). The plaque consists of fatty substances called lipids, which include cholesterol, cellular waste products, calcium, and fibrin (a blood-clotting material). As the plaque builds up, the artery walls become thicker, which may partially or totally block the lumen, thus restricting blood flow to and from the heart.

Sometimes, this layer of plaque breaks open and a blood clot forms to seal the break. Although a clot is a positive thing when you get a cut, this is not so in the case of arteries. In fact, it just makes things worse. As this cycle (fatty buildup, plaque rupture, and clot formation) continues, the arteries continue to narrow—which reduces the amount of blood that can pass through.

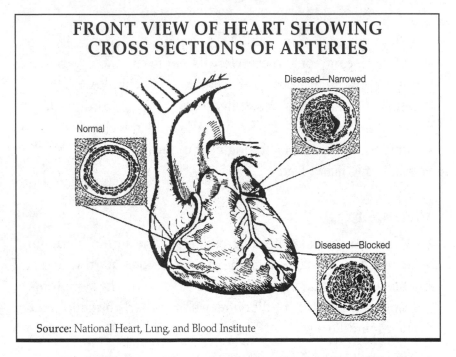

FRONT VIEW OF HEART SHOWING CROSS SECTIONS OF ARTERIES

Diseased—Narrowed

Normal

Diseased—Blocked

Source: National Heart, Lung, and Blood Institute

As I mentioned in Chapter 1, there are several *possible* contributors to this cycle; most researchers agree, however, that the following are the top three.

- high blood pressure
- high blood-cholesterol and triglyceride levels
- smoking

High Blood Pressure

In early 2002, the National Heart, Lung, and Blood Institute (NHLBI) released the findings of a study it supported on high blood pressure (HBP). Among other things, researchers stated that middle-aged Americans face a 90 percent chance of developing HBP at some time during the rest of their lives. Those who already have it also have some degree of atherosclerosis. Here's how one causes the other.

The force of the blood pushing against the arteries as it travels through the circulatory system is called **blood pressure**. HBP, or hypertension, occurs when the artery walls become thicker from plaque. When this occurs, the heart must work harder to get the blood to flow properly through the narrowed arteries. The harder the heart pumps to achieve this, the stronger the force or pressure is on the artery walls.

Hypertension is a major cardiovascular disease. In fact, one in every five Americans now has it. The number of deaths directly linked to hypertension has increased by 40 percent in the last 10 years, despite advances in blood pressure medications and home-monitoring devices. However, on the positive side, many researchers believe that the effective treatment of high blood pressure is a key reason for the accelerated decline in the death rates for stroke.

Although more than 32 percent of the population suffers from hypertension, the disease often carries no symptoms. This is why it's often called the "silent killer." A few symptoms that do <u>sometimes</u> appear are a pounding feeling in the head or chest, weakness, lightheadedness, and dizziness.

The best way to uncover this problem is to have your blood pressure checked regularly. With a **blood-pressure cuff**, a health-care professional will measure two forces: systolic pressure and diastolic pressure. The *systolic pressure* is the force of the blood when the heart contracts to pump blood out to the rest of the body. The heart relaxes between beats, and the pressure drops to its lowest point before a new beat. This force is the *diastolic pressure.*

A blood-pressure reading consists of these two numbers, which measure millimeters of mercury (mm Hg). They show how high the pressure inside your arteries can raise a column of mercury. For example, a person with a reading of 120/80 has a systolic pressure of 120 mm Hg and a diastolic pressure of 80 mm Hg. This is considered a *normal* blood-pressure reading for an adult, while a reading of 90/60 is considered low.

Although low blood pressure may be a sign of good physical fitness and low stress on the cardiovascular system, it also can cause unwanted symptoms, such as, for example, dizziness, fainting, difficulty in concentrating, blurred vision, and headaches. These could be signs of a more serious problem and should be checked out by a health-care practitioner.

At the other end of the spectrum, a reading of 140/90 is considered *high* for adults. According to researchers with the FHS, about one-half of the people who have a first heart attack and two-thirds of those who have a first stroke have blood-pressure readings higher than 160/95 mm HG.

When the heart has to work harder due to the presence of atherosclerosis, it becomes, as stated above, enlarged. The bigger the heart, the more difficult it is to maintain blood flow. Without the proper amount of oxygen, our bodies feel weak and tired and we cannot exercise or perform physical activities. Without treatment, our hearts may fail. (For more on this, see page 44 under "Congestive Heart Failure.")

Hypertension not only raises one's chances of a heart attack or stroke but also leads on occasion to kidney damage and problems with eyesight, particularly for those with diabetes.

Between the normal and the high readings, there is a category of *"high normal" blood pressure*—which is considered to be systolic pressure between 130 and 139 and diastolic pressure between 85 and 89. A recently published study showed that people with "high-normal" blood pressure are almost three times more likely to have heart attacks, strokes and heart failure than those with normal levels.

Beware "White-coat" Hypertension. Over the last several years, researchers have found that the blood-pressure readings of certain people rise when they are in a physician's office. This is called **white-coat hypertension**. A team of Italian researchers recently published findings of a study that showed this type of HBP to be more serious than previously believed.

Dr. Anna M. Grandi and colleagues at the University of Insubria in Varese, Italy, reported that patients with white-coat HBP showed signs of heart damage similar to but not as severe as the chronic condition. Previously, researchers only evaluated whether white-coat hypertension is a harmless condition or a sign of heart disease that should be treated.

Grandi and colleagues believe that it is not a harmless condition. The jury is still out on whether patients should be treated based on in-office BP readings or not, and more research is needed.

High Blood-cholesterol and Triglyceride Levels

Most of us already know that **cholesterol** is a fat like substance called a lipid and that having too much of it in our blood is a bad thing if we want to keep our hearts healthy.

Research has proven repeatedly that individuals with low levels of cholesterol and other fatty substances in their blood also have a low incidence of atherosclerosis and coronary heart disease.

But cholesterol is not bad in and of itself. In fact, our bodies need cholesterol to form cell membranes and make certain hormones. Our livers generally take care of that by manufacturing just the amount of cholesterol we need. It is the *extra* cholesterol that enters our bodies when we eat foods that come from animals (including meats, eggs, and dairy products) that causes high levels in the blood.

Scientists have studied the makeup and function of cholesterol for years. What they have discovered helps us understand how a substance that's so important for our body's basic functions can cause us such grief when we get too much of this good thing.

Cholesterol and other fats can't dissolve in the blood. As a result, special carriers called *lipoproteins* transport them via the bloodstream to the cells and back to the liver. *Low-density lipoproteins (LDL)*, which tend to fall apart, stick to artery walls and contribute to plaque build-up. There's little doubt that these "bad guys" are very big contributors to heart problems.

High-density lipoproteins (HDL) are more stable than LDLs and do not stick to artery walls. They transport the cholesterol back to the liver, where it's removed from the body. Because HDL keeps plaque from building up in the arteries, it's known as the "good" cholesterol. One way to keep the two straight is to connect the H in HDL to the word "healthy." Having a high HDL level is a healthy thing for your heart.

Getting one's blood cholesterol checked on an annual basis is just as important as having one's blood pressure measured regularly. Chapter 3 provides more information on cholesterol testing and results.

Triglycerides are another type of fat that exists naturally in the body as well as in food. People with high triglyceride levels often (but not always) have high levels of total cholesterol and LDL cholesterol and a low level of HDL cholesterol. This is an especially dangerous combination, and one that puts people at higher risk of developing heart problems. Recently, researchers also have linked high levels of these fats to a 30 percent increase in the risk of a stroke.

Generally, physicians treat high levels of triglycerides just as they do high levels of cholesterol. That is, they first suggest changes in diet and exercise habits.

A special message for women. According to the American Heart Association, women generally have higher HDL cholesterol levels during premenopausal years. The reason is that estrogen tends to raise HDL cholesterol levels, which protects women from heart disease. When estrogen drops after menopause, however, the risk of heart disease rises.

There's a lot of talk about how hormone-replacement therapy (HRT) addresses the risk of heart disease. However, the AHA cites recent clinical trials confirming that HRT does *not* appear to reduce the risks of cardiovascular disease and stroke in postmenopausal women. Treatment for women and men should be the same, with a focused effort on a better diet and more exercise.

Smoking

About 27 percent of American men and 22 percent of American women are smokers. Some researchers consider smoking to be *the* No. 1 risk factor for cardiovascular disease.

Although nicotine is the primary active agent in cigarette smoke, other chemicals and compounds (such as tar and carbon monoxide) are also present and harmful. The chemicals in tobacco smoke lead to the build-up of fatty plaque in the arteries, possibly by injuring the vessel walls. They also affect cholesterol and levels of fibrin (a blood-clotting material). This increases the risk of a blood clot that can lead to a heart attack.

Here are a few frightening facts on smoking from the National Heart, Lung, and Blood Institute (NHLBI) that should give even the most hardened smoker something to think about.

- About one in five deaths from overall CVD is attributable to smoking.
- The risk of a smoker having a heart attack is double that of a nonsmoker.
- Cigarette smoking is the biggest risk factor for sudden cardiac death.
- A smoker's risk of a heart attack is cut in half after only one year without smoking.
- Smokers who have heart attacks are more likely to die and die suddenly (within an hour) than are nonsmokers.

In recent years, studies have shown cigarette smoking also to be an important risk factor for stroke. People who smoke cigars or pipes have a higher risk of CHD (and possibly stroke) than that of nonsmokers, but their risk isn't as great as that of cigarette smokers.

Constant exposure to other people's smoke—called *environmental tobacco smoke, secondhand smoke,* or *passive smoking*—increases the risk of CHD even for nonsmokers. This increases by up to 30 percent among those exposed at home or work!

Smoking is considered a significant risk factor for women for yet another reason: It reduces the protective nature of estrogen. Research shows that women who smoke are 39 times more likely to have a heart attack and 22 times more likely to have a stroke than women who don't smoke.

Fortunately, despite all this dire information, World Health Organization (WHO) researchers say that just one year after quitting, the relative risk of dying from CHD for an ex-smoker approaches that of a longtime nonsmoker. Smoking cessation also dramatically lowers the risk of a heart attack and reduces the risk of a second one in people who've already had one.

Coronary Heart Disease

Hypertension is just the beginning of the problems that atherosclerosis causes. After high blood pressure, the most common one is coronary heart disease (CHD). AHA statistics show that CHD caused 48 percent of the deaths in the United States in 1998.

As mentioned above, the restriction or blockage caused by atherosclerosis may be a partial or a total one. A partial blockage *slows* the blood flow, which, in turn, *decreases* the oxygen reaching the heart. The lack of oxygen-rich blood is called *ischemia*, although many (20 percent to 30 percent) of those who experience this have no symptoms at all (a condition called *silent ischemia*).

Researchers from the NHLBI have found that among the earliest signs of CHD are chest pain (angina pectoris) and shortness of breath. These often occur following stress or after exercise.

For some, **arrhythmia** (an irregular heartbeat) may also occur—and this too can be silent. But silent or not, it is considered a precursor to a present or future diagnosis of heart disease.

A **heart attack** (again, sometimes silent and sometimes not) is one of the most common symptoms of CHD. A lengthy episode of ischemia also can trigger **cardiac arrest**, which means the heart suddenly stops beating, or **congestive heart failure**.

Depending upon who's doing the classifying, three of the above are considered "symptoms" of coronary heart disease: arrhythmia, angina, and heart attack. Congestive heart failure is a separate type of CVD. I discuss all of these in more detail below.

Arrhythmia

Any deviation from the normal pattern of one's heartbeat is called *arrhythmia*. In many cases, according to the medical community, an irregular heartbeat is not really "medically significant." Arrhythmia, in fact, is fairly common, and about one-fifth of healthy adults have frequent or multiple premature beats during just one day. While some occurrences are brief and unnoticeable, others are quite noticeable and signal the existence of a more serious problem. In severe cases, arrhythmia can lead to cardiac arrest and death.

As mentioned in the first chapter, each of the heart's contractions, or heartbeats, is triggered by electrical impulses that start in the sinoatrial (SA) node (the heart's natural pacemaker). The impulses travel from the SA node (in the upper-right part of the heart) through the rest of the chambers to trigger and regulate the heartbeat. Any problems along this pathway (known as the **conduction system)** could cause an irregular heartbeat.

The main causes of arrhythmia are atherosclerosis, high blood pressure, and inflammatory or degenerative conditions. The scarring or abnormal tissue deposits that occur with these conditions

---

W A R N I N G   S I G N S   O F   A R R H Y T H M I A

Although symptoms vary widely, the following are the most commonly experienced:

- palpitations (a strong or galloping heartbeat)

- skipped heartbeats

- dizziness, fatigue, or fainting as a result of the brain's not getting enough oxygen

- angina

- shortness of breath

---

can interfere with the work of the SA node or the overall conduction system, which can cause *bradycardia* (a slow heartbeat) or *tachycardia* (a fast heartbeat). Although an arrhythmia may last only for a few seconds, it also may last for several minutes or even hours and cause serious injury to organs other than the heart. The most successful way of restoring natural rhythm is through electric shock to the heart via use of a machine called a *defibrillator.*

Blood flow that's blocked for an extended time also may cause **atrial fibrillation** (AF)—rapid, random contractions of the **atria** (the two small upper chambers of the heart). Since the heart is not pumping properly during this time, oxygen-rich blood may not completely leave the left atrium when the heart beats but instead pool and clot. If a piece of the resulting clot breaks free, it can enter into the circulation and lodge in a narrowed artery. This, of course,

---

AT RISK OF ARRHYTHMIA

Gender and age affect the chances of a person's experiencing atrial fibrillation and the level of its severity. Men are slightly more likely than women to develop it, but women diagnosed with it carry a longer-term risk of premature death. As with many things, the chance of arrhythmia tends to increase with age—even when there's no clear sign of heart disease.

Atrial fibrillation often shows up in people who have had coronary heart disease, a heart attack, or heart failure. It's also found in those with heart-valve disease, those with an inflamed heart muscle or lining (endocarditis), and those who've had recent heart surgery. People with atherosclerosis and angina sometimes have it, and sometimes it's related to congenital heart defects or lung problems.

Addictive substances—especially alcohol, cigarettes, and recreational drugs (especially stimulants)—can provoke irregular heartbeats, as can various cardiac medications. The AHA says that even drugs used to treat an arrhythmia may actually cause another arrhythmia.

The risk also increases for those with thyroid disorders, diabetes, and high blood pressure.

causes problems, such as stroke. (See "Types of Strokes" page 46) About 15 percent of strokes occur in people with atrial fibrillation, according to the American Stroke Association.

An arrhythmia also may cause *ventricular tachycardia* and *ventricular fibrillation*, extremely fast, chaotic rhythms during which the lower chambers quiver, rather than beat, and the heart can't pump any blood. The result could be a cardiac arrest unless medical help is provided immediately.

Angina Pectoris

We never hear someone say they are experiencing "angina pectoris"—a Latin phrase that means "strangling in the chest." What we do hear is that they are having chest pain, and this pain can range from mild to severe. Usually, an attack lasts no more than a few minutes and occurs because the heart is not getting enough oxygenated blood. The reason is, of course, a partially blocked artery (usually caused by atherosclerosis).

Most cases involve **stable angina,** which is predictable chest pain that occurs during physical exertion and subsides when the activity stops. Extreme cold or hot temperatures, heavy meals, alcohol, and smoking also may trigger stable angina. There are also, however, some cases of **unstable angina**, which refers to unexpected chest pain while at rest.

Angina attacks experienced by men usually occur after the age of 30 and almost always are caused by coronary artery disease, according to the AHA. For women, however, angina tends to occur later in life and may be caused by other reasons, including those below.

■ *aortic stenosis*: narrowing of the aortic valve in the heart that obstructs the flow of blood from the left ventricle into the aorta

> **WARNING SIGNS OF ANGINA**
>
> One sign is a severe squeezing, suffocating, or burning feeling that tends to begin in the center of the chest underneath the breastbone. The pain may spread to the left shoulder, into the teeth and jaw area, and sometimes even into the wrist. Some people say they feel numbness or loss of sensation in their arms, shoulders, or wrists.
>
> The following also are considered angina symptoms, although not as consistently reported as the above.
>
> ✔ nausea or an upset stomach
>
> ✔ severe sweating
>
> ✔ weakness, tiredness, and/or fatigue
>
> ✔ an indigestion-type feeling in the upper abdomen

- *anemia*: a disorder characterized by a decrease in hemoglobin in the blood to below normal, decreased red-blood production or increased red-blood-cell destruction, or blood loss
- *hyperthyroidism*: an overactive thyroid gland

According to experts, a person with angina is more likely to have a heart attack than someone who has never experienced it.

Heart Attacks

Some individuals don't ever experience angina, and their first outward symptom of coronary artery disease may be a heart attack (medically known as a ***myocardial infarction***). According to AHA statistics, 38 percent of women and 25 percent of men die within a year after a heart attack unless lifestyle changes are made.

A heart attack occurs when blood flow to the heart is totally blocked and the heart does not receive enough oxygen. Although the heart is still beating during a heart attack, the heart cells begin to die. The more time that passes without treatment, the greater the damage.

WARNING SIGNS OF A HEART ATTACK

Discomfort that occurs in the center of the chest and lasts for more than a few minutes, or goes away and comes back. This can feel like uncomfortable pressure, squeezing, fullness, or pain.

Discomfort in other areas of the upper body. This includes pain in one or both arms or in the back, neck, jaw, or stomach.

Shortness of breath. This often occurs at the same time as chest discomfort, but it also can occur before chest discomfort. Women tend to experience it more often than men do.

Other symptoms. A cold sweat, nausea, or lightheadedness may also occur.

Many heart attacks start slowly, such as with a mild pain or slight discomfort. The symptoms may come and go, and those who have already had a heart attack may experience different symptoms the second time around. (See "Warning Signs of a Heart Attack" above.)

Thousands of heart-attack victims wait hours after experiencing the symptoms to seek help. Some actually wait days, as the symptoms increase in severity, before they take action. Many even drive themselves to the hospital for assistance.

Gender Differences

Researchers from the Framingham Heart Study discovered that CHD manifests itself differently in men and women. In women, the most common initial symptom is angina; in men, however, it is a myocardial infarction. Women with angina fare better than their male counterparts because men have more underlying heart disease. However, women with angina have five times the risk of future coronary events that those free of angina have.

According to Dr. Denton A. Cooley, president, surgeon-in-chief, and founder of the Texas Heart Institute in Houston, "Women usually develop heart disease about a decade later than men. Men tend to show signs of heart disease in their 40s and 50s. As women age, their risk for heart disease markedly increases. This is probably due to the decreasing estrogen levels during and after menopause."

According to Cooley and other researchers, medical studies indicate that estrogen protects young women against heart attacks by increasing the high-density lipoprotein (HDL) cholesterol levels in the blood. HDL cholesterol, in turn, helps prevent plaque from collecting in the arteries.

"Heart disease poses the biggest threat to the average woman's life," says Dr. Cooley. "Postmenopausal women may be able to reduce the risk of cardiovascular disease by taking estrogen or hormone-replacement therapy." However, this may not be the way some women want to go—and there are alternatives, such as eating more foods high in tofu and other herbal supplements.

For both sexes, it is generally believed that, for several reasons, the risk of developing heart disease increases with age. Our arteries become stiff, for example, and the heart walls thicken. Also, the heart muscles may not relax as fully as they once did; because of this, the heart's ability to pump blood to muscles drops, which, in turn, increases the likelihood of acquiring cardiovascular disease. However, as I've described in Chapter 6, new findings from the University of Pittsburgh's Graduate School of Public Health show that people who are more physically active and who have normal blood-sugar levels also suffer less from stiff arteries.

Congestive Heart Failure

The term "heart failure" may sound as if it is referring to a heart that has stopped, but it isn't. It is used to explain that the heart is not pumping enough blood in relation to the amount returning to the lungs and in relation to the body's metabolic requirements.

W A R N I N G   S I G N S   O F   C H F

Left-sided heart failure. The symptoms include difficulty in breathing and a "bubbling" sound on exhalation or inhalation. Fatigue may also be a symptom.

Right-sided heart failure. Complaints of a persistent cold, a dry cough, and wheezing may arise. Many times, these symptoms are mistaken for those of an allergic reaction.

Usually, congestive heart failure develops over a number of years. As we age, the heart gradually loses its pumping capacity and works less efficiently. The seriousness of the condition depends, of course, on how much capacity is lost. But after the age of 40, CHF frequently signals an underlying heart problem, particularly coronary atherosclerois with myocardial infarction, as well as valvular heart disease and other problems.

This cardiovascular disease generally occurs as either **left-sided heart failure** or **right-sided heart failure.** When the *left side* of the heart is affected, blood accumulates in the veins instead of being carried from the lungs and thus causes the lungs to fill with fluid. In the case of *right-sided heart failure,* blood accumulates in the veins leading from the body back to the heart. This causes swelling in the lower body parts (including the feet and legs).

Peripheral Vascular Disease

The May 2001 guidelines released by the National Cholesterol

Education Program (NCEP) include a special mention of patients with diseases occurring in blood vessels in areas of the body other than the heart. These occur in the peripheral blood vessels in our feet, legs, lower arms, neck, or head.

Peripheral artery disease, like coronary heart disease, involves atherosclerosis, particularly in the carotid arteries (the main arteries carrying oxygen to the brain). Carotid-artery disease significantly increases the risk of having an *ischemic stroke*—the most common type of stroke. *Peripheral venous disorders*, such as varicose veins, constitute another type of vascular disease.

In its guidelines, the NCEP recommends that patients with these diseases be just as vigilant in controlling blood-lipid levels as those with other coronary-artery and heart disease. Physicians should treat them according to the same guidelines as used with heart-disease patients.

Stroke

People with heart problems, particularly those with a history of arrhythmia, have more than twice the risk of suffering a stroke. The risk factors listed for heart disease are considered secondary risk factors for stroke: high blood cholesterol and trigylcerides, physical inactivity, and excessive weight. (In other words, they increase the risk of heart disease, which, in turn, increases the risk of suffering a stroke.) Heart attacks constitute the major cause of death among stroke survivors.

According to the American Stroke Association (ASA), someone in the United States has a stroke every 53 seconds and someone dies of one every 3.3 minutes. Most of these people are under 65, and, according to the FHS, females account for almost 62 percent of the deaths from stroke. It's the nation's third-leading cause of death, ranking behind all the other cardiovascular diseases and all forms of cancer. It is a leading cause of serious, long-term disability.

Like the other conditions I have discussed, atherosclerosis plays a role in stroke. The biggest difference, however, is that the plaque build-up blocks the blood flow through the **carotid arteries** (vessels supplying the brain with oxygen and nutrients) instead of the coronary arteries in the heart.

A stroke occurs when a vessel bursts or is clogged by a blood clot or some other particle. Because of the rupture, a part of the brain doesn't get the flow of blood needed. Within just a few minutes, nerve cells in that part of the brain die and the part of the body that the cells control also dies. Because dead brain cells aren't replaceable, the effects of a stroke are often permanent.

There are four major types of strokes. Blood clots (thrombus) or particles that plug an artery cause *cerebral thrombosis* and *cerebral embolism*. These two types are the most common, accounting for about 70 percent to 80 percent of all incidents. They also carry a lower fatality rate than do the other two—*cerebral hemorrhages* and *subarachnoid hemorrhages*, which are caused by ruptured blood vessels (or hemorrhage).

W A R N I N G   S I G N S   O F   A   S T R O K E

If you notice one or more of these symptoms in yourself or another person, get to a hospital immediately. In the case of a stroke, every second really does count. Treatment is more effective if provided soon after a stroke occurs.

- sudden numbness or weakness of the face, arm, or leg, especially on one side of the body
- sudden confusion, difficulty in speaking or understanding
- sudden trouble in seeing with one or both eyes
- sudden difficulty walking, dizziness, loss of balance, or loss of coordination
- sudden, severe headaches with no known cause

Many of us are familiar with *transient ischemic attacks (TIAs)*, or "ministrokes," which often precede one of the major types of stroke. These recurrent episodes, which produce stroke-type symptoms, can last from several seconds to several hours. TIAs are strong predictors of an imminent stroke, so it's important to get medical help immediately. According to the ASA, someone who's had one or more TIAs is almost 10 times more likely to have a stroke than someone of the same age and sex who hasn't.

Effects of a stroke. It's a bit of an understatement to say that the brain is an extremely complex organ. As already mentioned, it is the control center for many body functions. The effects of a stroke depend primarily on the location of the obstruction and the extent of brain tissue affected. One thing that's always true is that one side of the brain controls the opposite side of the body.

If for example, the stroke occurs in the brain's right side, the left side of the body (and the right side of the face) will be affected. Results could include paralysis on the left side, vision problems, and memory loss. If the stroke occurs in the left side, the right side of the body (and left side of the face) will be affected. Some or all of the following could occur as the result of a stroke.

- paralysis
- speech/language problems
- memory loss

Some people have strokes and recover completely within a few days, while others may never recover. The severity of a stroke depends upon the part of the brain that's affected, the extent of the damage, how quickly the body restores blood to the injured parts of the brain, and how quickly the healthy parts of the brain can take over for the injured parts.

• CHAPTER 3 •

Modern Medicine's Approach to Heart Disease

As much as we would like to do without it, many of us would not be alive without the help of modern medicine. More often than not, drug therapies and surgical procedures *do* help fix what's broken—in the heart and elsewhere. But like everything and everyone else, modern medicine and its practitioners are not perfect. There's even a special word for the imperfections that occur in the world of medicine: *iatrogenic.*

An iatrogenic complication or disorder is one that is actually **caused** by treatment or diagnostic procedures, by medical personnel, or by being exposed to a health-care environment. Some of these complications are minor, but others are life-threatening. Their causes vary widely, but clinical error has been cited as the reason for at least half of these events.

I bring this up not to criticize the medical world but to emphasize that some of these iatrogenic problems might not occur if we, as health-care consumers, paid more attention and made more of a commitment to being in control of our own health care. As you read the information provided in this chapter, it will become abundantly clear that you will want to stay alert to the decisions physicians are making about your health and that of your loved ones.

I've already said it, but I can't repeat it enough. Share the responsibility for your health and heart care with your physicians and other medical providers. If you are at risk of heart disease, or already have been diagnosed with it, you might need one of the procedures or drugs discussed below. Should that occur, it will be important that you know everything you can about the drug or procedure in question before you use it or undergo it. What you'll find below is a brief introduction to some of the scientific options that are available.

Preventive Aspirin Therapy

I assume you are familiar with the old adage "an apple a day keeps the doctor away." Many experts are now saying that although it does have a nice ring to it, it now warrants a new twist; an aspirin a day keeps a heart attack away. Researchers began studying *aspirin therapy* in the early 1970s, and it's now practically mainstream.

The official word came from the U.S. Preventive Services Task Force, which was convened by a division of the Department of Health and Human Services. The Jan. 15, 2002, issue of the *Annals of Internal Medicine* contained the task force's suggestion that using aspirin on a regular basis can *prevent* a heart attack in individuals who have never had a heart attack or stroke but who are in a high-risk category.

After reviewing a volume of "well-designed, well-conducted" studies completed over a 35-year period, the task force concluded that the evidence was "good" (its highest grade) that the benefits of aspirin therapy outweigh its risks. In fact, the data showed that it reduced the risk for a heart attack by an average of 28 percent.

In general, aspirin works best with individuals whose blood-pressure, cholesterol, and weight levels are within the normal range. Studies cite that the following groups of people can benefit the most from aspirin therapy: men over 40, postmenopausal women, and younger people with coronary-heart-disease risk factors. Although the best dosage has not been conclusively decided upon, low dosages of about 75 mg per day seem to be as effective as higher amounts.

According to Dr. Roger S. Blumenthal, director of preventive cardiology at Johns Hopkins University in Baltimore, Maryland, "One of the things the task force wanted to get across is that the easiest and most cost-efficient intervention to lower one's risk of cardiovascular disease is low-dose aspirin."

The fact that aspirin is easy to acquire, the fact that it is reasonably priced, and the fact that it is effective are important points. So is the fact that the benefits of taking it outweigh the risks. As you'll see below, there are other, more expensive prescription drugs that solve the same problem but don't offer the same advantages.

However, before starting aspirin therapy, check with your physician, who should perform a risk assessment involving such factors as age, sex, diabetes, elevated total-cholesterol levels, low levels of high-density lipoprotein cholesterol, elevated blood pressure, family history, and smoking. In addition, some people would not be candidates because they are allergic to aspirin or have other conditions that aren't compatible with it. Only after these things are checked should someone begin aspirin therapy.

Although the task force's recommendation is an important milestone, many physicians and professional organizations have recommended aspirin therapy for years. For example, in 2000, the American Diabetes Association recommended that clinicians consider aspirin for primary prevention of heart disease in diabetic patients who are older than 30 or have cardiovascular-disease risk factors and no problems with aspirin usage. The European Society of Cardiology weighed in on the subject even earlier, in 1998, when it recommended low doses for patients with well-controlled hypertension and men at a previously high risk for CHD.

As long ago as 1997, the American Heart Association concluded that aspirin *might* be warranted for high-risk patients. It recently clarified this by saying that daily aspirin is recommended for "patients who have experienced a myocardial infarction (heart attack), unstable angina, an ischemic stroke, or transient ischemic attacks (TIAs, or little strokes) if not contraindicated." People who have not experienced any of these cardiovascular problems should consult their physicians, the AHA stated.

How Aspirin Works

As explained in Chapter 2, clots can block blood flow through the coronary arteries to the heart and trigger a heart attack and can obstruct the carotid arteries going to the brain and cause a stroke. Aspirin stops blood platelets from sticking together, and this, in turn, prevents blood clots from forming. Aspirin's ability to stop the clotting is what makes it so important.

In fact, a 1997 study published by the AHA reported that up to 10,000 more people would survive heart attacks each year if they took one aspirin tablet at the first sign of the attack. Of the 1.25 million Americans per year who have heart attacks, only 60 percent to 80 percent of them currently receive aspirin while in cardiac crisis.

Even those who are having a heart attack can benefit from aspirin. Immediately after calling 911, heart-attack victims should *chew* a tablet of regular adult aspirin (325 milligrams) or four baby aspirins (324 milligrams) to halt the clotting that's causing the attack. Although this may not prevent all of the damage, it is believed that it will minimize it. (Note that the aspirin should be *chewed*, instead of swallowed, to allow it reach the bloodstream more quickly.)

Know the Risks

Although aspirin does have amazing properties, it is not the answer for everyone. As with any medication, it's essential to discuss this option with your own physician to determine any special risks or side effects—and some are quite possible.

First, there are the risks mentioned in the task force's clinical guidelines. Specifically, there is "good" evidence that aspirin when taken for five years or more increases the incidence of major *gastrointestinal-bleeding episodes*. That increase is 2 percent to 4 percent in middle-aged people and 4 percent to 12 percent in those that are older. There also is a slight increase in the incidence of hemorrhagic strokes (or bleeding in the brain) for those age groups. When aspirin was taken for five or more years, the incidence of stroke increased about 2 percent.

There also are the risks associated with aspirin's classification as a nonsteroidal anti-inflammatory drug (NSAID).

The NSAID-Aspirin Connection. NSAIDs are often the first choice in the general population for reducing pain and treating inflammation, because, in medical lingo, they are "well-tolerated" (which means they usually don't give people much trouble). However, with extended use (such as that required in aspirin therapy), they often cause stomach discomfort, and they sometimes cause internal bleeding.

People who are allergic to aspirin should obviously avoid it. Others who should avoid it include those who suffer from asthma or high blood pressure. Furthermore, recent studies have suggested that elderly heart patients who take frequent high doses of NSAIDs may be up to 10 times as likely to develop heart failure as those not taking them.

In general, health providers usually advise older adults to take low doses of NSAIDs and to take them less frequently. Older patients with a medical history of heart disease should talk with their physicians before taking any NSAIDs at all.

The list of reasons (in addition to the above) why a person would not be a candidate for going on aspirin therapy is long. Although some of the more common reasons, including risks and side effects, are listed below, talking to your doctor about your individual situation is a must.

- Heavy drinkers (those who consume three or more drinks per day) should not take aspirin, because it has been linked to stomach irritation, liver damage, and excessive bleeding.
- Anyone suffering from chronic intestinal problems should not be on aspirin therapy.
- Regular use can increase the risk of cataracts, particularly among patients under the age of 65, so those with a personal or family medical history of this condition may not be candidates.
- If you're going to undergo surgery, you should refrain from taking aspirin for several days (generally 10) before the procedure.

In these and other questionable cases, providers may prescribe one of the blood-thinning (or anticlotting) medicines instead of aspirin. Information about these can be found below under the heading "Prescription-drug Therapies."

Drug Interactions. Of particular concern is mixing aspirin with antihypertensives and anticoagulants. *Antihypertensives* are prescribed to treat high blood pressure, and taking any type of NSAID with them may reduce their effectiveness. Mixing *anticoagulants* (or anticlotting medications, such as coumadin) with aspirin may raise the risk of excessive bleeding. There is even some evidence that taking vitamin E or omega-3 fatty-acid supplements with NSAIDs may increase a person's tendency toward internal bleeding.

Drinking grapefruit juice may interfere with the liver's ability to rid the body of some NSAIDs, which could lead to a build-up of toxins. While such an accumulation is less likely if the juice is ingested four or more hours prior to the medicine, patients taking NSAIDs are often advised to refrain from drinking grapefruit juice. (Note, however, that there is no indication that eating grapefruit presents any danger.)

A study published in the *New England Journal of Medicine* in 2001 warned against mixing ibuprofen (another NSAID) with aspirin because the combination appears to undermine the anticlotting mechanism. Dr. Garret A. Fitzgerald and colleagues from the University of Pennsylvania found that other painkillers in the NSAIDs category did not have this effect. Fitzgerald advised patients who take aspirin to protect their hearts to ask their physicians for an alternative painkiller.

Diagnosing the Problem

Individuals who have experienced symptoms of cardiovascular disease (CVD) should see their physicians. As described in Chapter 2, the following are the most serious symptoms.

- chest pain (angina)
- heart attack

■ arrhythmia

Those being evaluated for heart problems should first share their medical history with their respective doctors and then receive a physical exam. A doctor will ordinarily order tests to help diagnose the problem. Which tests will be ordered will depend upon several things—including the patient's risk factors, history of heart problems, and current symptoms—and the physician's interpretation of those factors.

People being evaluated for possible heart disease are usually given simple tests first. Initially, blood tests are ordered to confirm or rule out the presence of certain cardiac enzymes (or markers of heart damage). The physician may order a chest X-ray, an electrocardiogram (ECG), an exercise stress test, or all three. (See page 58 for more on these.)

Depending on what the doctor finds, more complicated diagnostic tests may be ordered. Echocardiographies, computed tomography (CT) scans, and magnetic-resonance-imaging tests are the most common ones.

The results of these diagnostic tests can help your doctor isolate the source of the problem. For people who already have heart disease (such as someone who's had a heart attack) or have had previous surgeries, diagnostic tests can show whether the disease is under control.

Most tests used to detect CVD are known as *imaging procedures,* because they take X-rays of the heart. Although these images may not look like much to us, radiologists (physicians who specialize in these procedures) understand the message behind them, and it's their job to interpret that message to decide upon the next steps, which may include prescription-drug treatments and/or surgical intervention.

The bottom line is that there are a number of tests available and only a doctor can decide which one is best for you if you are experiencing heart-related problems. Most of these tests are designed to show one or more of the following:

- the structure and function of the heart and the blood flow within it
- electrical problems within the heart
- circulatory problems in the coronary arteries

Many heart problems can be detected with tests that are *noninvasive*, or performed on the surface of the body. Sometimes, though, more detailed investigation will be required and the physician will order one or more of the numerous *invasive tests* available. These ordinarily involve the insertion of a contrast medium (special dye), needles, or instruments.

Basic Tests First

As you'll see, there are many options available to uncover whether or not a person has CVD and how bad it is. Let's start out with a quick look at some basic, and common, diagnostic tests.

Cholesterol Testing

Having one's cholesterol level tested has become standard fare in an annual physical exam. For a cholesterol-screening test, blood is drawn from a vein or through a fingertip "prick" test. Most health-care professionals believe that blood drawn from a vein provides more accurate readings.

For the most complete and accurate results, the best place to have blood drawn and tests run is a medical facility or clinic and not one of the screening clinics often set up in malls and public places. Home-testing devices are highly questionable, because these do not measure HDL levels and, therefore, don't provide total-cholesterol readings.

A blood test is used to measure the milligrams (mg) of cholesterol per deciliter (dL) of blood. The results of your cholesterol test can act as a map to determine your risk of heart disease. The standard test measures total-cholesterol and HDL levels only, but a *lipopro-*

GUIDELINES FOR HEALTHY CHOLESTEROL LEVELS

In May 2001, the National Cholesterol Education Program (of the National Heart, Lung, and Blood Institute) updated its guidelines for healthy levels of cholesterol. When you get your cholesterol test done, compare your levels with those in the box below to see where you fall.

Total cholesterol level	Category
less than 200 mg/dL	desirable
200-239 mg/dL	borderline high
240 mg/dL and above	high

LDL cholesterol level	Category
less than 100 mg/dL	optimal
100-129 mg/dL	near optimal/above optimal
130-159 mg/dL	borderline high
160-189 mg/dL	high
190 mg/dL and above	very high

HDL cholesterol level	Category
less than 40 mg/dL	low (increased risk)
60 mg/dL and higher	high (heart-protective)

Triglyceride level	Category
less than 150 mg/dL	normal
150 to 199 mg/dL	borderline high
200 to 499 mg/dL	high
500 mg/dL and higher	very high

Source: "High Blood Cholesterol: What You Need to Know," National Institutes of Health, National Heart, Lung, and Blood Institute, May 2001

---

tein profile (which requires a nine- to 12-hour fast before blood is drawn) is a more comprehensive test—and it is recommended that your doctor order it for you every five years. The profile includes information about LDL, HDL, total-cholesterol, and trigylceride levels.

You can get even more information about your risk of heart disease by knowing the *ratio* of total cholesterol to HDL cholesterol in addition to knowing the cholesterol levels. To get the ratio, divide the total-cholesterol value by the HDL cholesterol value. A number higher than 5 shows an increased risk in people who do not have heart disease. People who already have heart disease should not have a number higher than 4.

A Chest X-ray

If you've made it to adulthood, you've probably had an X-ray of some sort—and a chest X-ray isn't much different from any other kind. It is, however, unique in the sense that it's the only X-ray that produces an image of the heart as well as the large arteries and their surroundings. The physician uses the images from the X-ray to see if any abnormalities exist. A chest X-ray may show, for example, an enlarged heart.

An Electrocardiogram

The first test your physician orders may be an electrocardiogram (ECG or EKG). Once you're hooked up to the machine, the ECG picks up the electrical energy or impulses going through the heart and records them on a moving strip of paper. Physicians "read" the ECG strip to get information about the heart's activity, such as whether its rate and rhythm are normal, and to decide if further tests are needed.

The ECG could turn out normal even when a person is having

obvious heart problems. If that's the case, the patient may need to wear a *Holter monitor* over the shoulder or around the waist so that an ambulatory ECG may be done. This battery-powered device includes a cassette tape that records the heart's rate and rhythm for at least 24 hours. The only thing patients must do is keep a list of their daily activities and the times they are performed. The physician compares this list with the monitor output to see what activity triggered abnormal readings.

An Exercise Stress Test

While the ECG monitors the heart at rest, this test monitors a heart at work. While hooked up to an ECG, the patient begins walking on a treadmill or bicycling on a stationary machine. The speed and elevation are continuously increased to mimic the experience of going up a small hill. During this activity, a person's heart rate, blood pressure, breathing, and level of tiredness are measured. The test can show whether enough blood and oxygen are being pumped to the heart during physical exertion.

There are several variations of the exercise stress test. For example, there's the *nuclear (thallium) stress test* that starts with the standard exercise stress test. The patient then receives injections of contrast medium and lies down on a special table beneath a gamma camera that take pictures of the contrast rushing through the blood. Another type is the *stress echocardiography*, which combines the exercise stress test with echocardiography. (See next page.)

For healthy people, taking the exercise stress test will be no more difficult than walking up a small hill. Those with hearts that aren't functioning properly may have more trouble, but they will be watched closely and treated if they experience problems.

Echocardiography

For professionals who know what they're looking at, the "echo" produced in this procedure is like a movie of the cardio-vascular system—and all the patient has to do is lie on a table. To start the "movie," a technician passes a wandlike device called a transducer over the body; this transducer sends high-frequency sound waves (ultrasound) into the chest. These waves bounce off the heart's walls and valves and return as echoes. The echoes appear as multidimensional images on a television monitor.

Medical experts consider this to be an extremely valuable diag-nostic tool for a number of reasons. The echo not only reveals the heart's size, shape, texture, and movement but also shows the blood flow within the heart. If there's a blockage or narrowed artery, it often can be seen.

Computed Tomography (CT) Scans

CT scans provide still, clear images of the heart, lungs, and blood vessels. Many people mistakenly call this procedure a "CAT scan," but, technically speaking, a CAT scan is a computerized axial tomography (CAT) scan, which examines the brain and its functions, not the heart.

A conventional CT scan is performed with the aid of a large, nar-row machine with a hole in the center and an X-ray tube inside. A patient lies down on a table that moves slowly through the hollow center of the scanner, and a device rotates around the patient while taking *hundreds* of X-rays of the heart area from different angles. A powerful computer software program then goes to work to reassem-ble those images into a cross-sectional view of the heart and blood vessels. There are several variations of this test, including the *Ultrafast*® *Electron Beam CT* (EBCT) and the *spiral (helical) CT*.

While a conventional CT scan takes an image within 10 seconds, the *EBCT* takes one in about a tenth of a second. Speed like this lowers the chance of blurred pictures caused by movement, such as the beating of the heart. The blurred picture is considered the major drawback of the conventional scan.

Another benefit of the EBCT is that it can detect and photograph calcium deposits in the coronary arteries, which a conventional scan cannot. The amount of calcium relates directly to the level of atherosclerosis present. But even the EBCT cannot show a blocked artery.

The *spiral (helical) CT's* claim to fame is its faster, higher-quality images. The speed is useful to elderly patients and those who are critically ill, because the length of time the scanning takes is often a problem. A spiral CT can be completed during a single breath hold.

Magnetic Resonance Imaging (MRI)

I once saw a coffee mug with "I survived my MRI" printed on it, but, in truth, there's nothing to fear from this procedure unless you suffer from claustrophobia. The machine used for MRI resembles the CT scanner; instead of being placed on a table that moves through the hollow center of a scanner, however, patients are placed on one that stays inside the tubelike scanner.

A powerful magnet is activated when the machine is turned on. This generates a magnetic field that is "roughly 10,000 times stronger than the Earth's," according to the National Institutes of Health. The atoms in the body react to the magnetic field and send back a faint radio signal. A computer hooked up to the MRI machine reads the signals and generates detailed two or three-dimensional images of the heart muscle.

In addition to those who suffer from claustrophobia, people with implanted metallic objects and cardiac pacemakers should not even get close to a MRI—because of the incredibly strong magnetic field.

Complex Tests for Complex Problems

The diagnostic procedures described above do not always show arteries as clearly as they might need to be shown for a diagnosis. To remedy this, a radioactive substance called a **contrast medium** can be injected into the patient's bloodstream via a thin, long, plastic tube called a **catheter.**

Using a *fluoroscope*, which is a device that projects a "real-time" image on a television monitor, the physician can actually see the blood flowing (or not flowing) through the arteries. The insertion of the tube into the artery or vein is known as a **cardiac catheterization.**

In spite of its diagnostic advantages, some people are allergic to the contrast medium injected. If you have any of the tests described below, be sure to tell your physician what medications and supplements you're taking and what, if any, other medical conditions you have. For example, people with kidney disease or diabetes are not good candidates for many of them.

Transesophageal Echocardiography (TEE)

Like the standard echocardiogram described above, the TEE uses high-frequency ultrasound to produce heart images. However, the TEE is definitely an invasive procedure—and here's why: The transducer is attached to a small, flexible, tubelike device (called a probe, or scope) that a patient swallows with help from an experienced technician.

The transducer ends up in the esophagus, where it is directed toward the heart. It picks up the sound-wave echoes and relays them to an echocardiograph that displays a two-dimensional picture of the heart and the aorta. The heart images are highly detailed, because they come from the *inside* of, rather than through, the chest wall.

The biggest drawback of the TEE is the discomfort that occurs when the transducer is inserted. Once it's in place, there "should not" be any pain—although a sore throat may follow the procedure.

Positron-emission Tomography (PET)

Numerous clinical studies have proven that PET scans have an important role in diagnosing patients, describing disease, and developing treatment strategies. PET scans are highly accurate in detecting, localizing, and describing coronary-artery disease and identifies injury, but still viable, heart muscle.

The PET scan differs from other scans in its use of radiation detectors. The detectors are strapped around the patient's chest, and the patient lies on a table that moves inside the PET scanner. The detectors measure the radioactivity being caused by the injected contrast medium, and pictures are taken of the heart. Because the type of radioactive substance used gravitates toward damaged tissue, physicians can identify problem areas quickly. As is the case with the CT scan, powerful computer software creates pictures of the heart at work and projects them onto a monitor.

Generally, a PET scan is considered one of the most accurate diagnostic tests, and its only real drawback may be possible claustrophobia from being in the closed scanner. Also, people with diabetes must have their blood-sugar levels monitored during the test to ensure that they remain constant.

Cardiac Catheterization

This test is useful in many ways, including the fact that many other procedures could not be performed without it. A small incision is made in the skin, and a catheter is inserted into an artery, a vein, or a heart chamber. An injection of a contrast medium allows the physician to view the heart's activity under fluoroscopy (live X-ray images). The steps that follow insertion of the catheter and injection of the dye vary, according to the procedure to be performed.

The catheter and the contrast allow the physician to visualize and measure blood pressure and flow *within* the heart. Physicians often use a cardiac catheter to decide whether a patient needs an angiogram or another surgical procedure. This procedure is also used for therapeutic purposes. If, for example, a blood clot is seen during an angiogram, the physician may inject certain drugs through the catheter to break it up.

Although it's one of the most commonly performed procedures, it also involves risks—some more serious than others. The National Institutes of Health lists a number of risks for cardiac catheterization. Included on the *"rare-but-it-can-happen"* list are arrhythmias, trauma to the vein or artery, low blood pressure, infections, embolism from a blood clot at the catheter tip, a negative reaction to the contrast medium, hemorrhage or hematoma at the site of catheter access, strokes, and heart attacks.

Electrophysiology Studies (EPS)

Using the EPS procedure, physicians can study patients with arrhythmias. After a catheter is inserted into the blood vessel, electronic signals are sent into the heart—which may cause an arrhythmia. Physicians can see the location of the arrhythmia and decide upon the appropriate follow-up to prevent or control future arrhythmias. They can, for example, experiment by injecting many different antiarrhythmic medications through the catheter to see which one stops the problem.

Intravascular Ultrasound (IVUS)

This procedure begins with a cardiac catheterization and proceeds to an advanced sort of echocardiography. The transducer is attached to the end of a catheter before it is inserted into a blood vessel. From inside the body, sound waves bounce off the heart walls and return as echoes; these then appear as images on a television monitor. Doctors can move the transducer around to take internal pictures from different angles. An IVUS is rarely performed alone or as a strictly diagnostic procedure but rather as a predecessor to a more complicated surgery.

A Coronary Angiogram

This X-ray procedure, which is often ordered after a diagnosis of atherosclerosis, allows the physician to see inside the blood vessels and study the blood flow and pressure of the coronary arteries. The angiogram begins with a cardiac catheterization and an injection of contrast medium into the artery closest to the heart. Several X-rays are taken of the blood flow and heart activity.

The images are stored in a computer, which displays the internal activity as if it were a movie. This allows physicians to evaluate the severity of abnormalities present, such as a narrowed or blocked vessel, that may cause angina or lead to a heart attack. Physicians consider an angiogram to be a sort of internal "map" that shows them the way to the proper treatment or surgery.

Coronary angiograms are considered to be among the most accurate tests for diagnosing coronary-artery disease. However, the medical literature is somewhat inconsistent about their safety.

Some sources say that complications are rare, with the most common risk being a reaction or allergy to the contrast medium. However, the AHA and the American College of Cardiology cite several possible complications, including arrhythmias, a stroke, a heart attack, and other, less-serious, problems. In spite of the risks, over a million coronary angiograms are performed each year because of the benefits offered by the procedure.

Researchers have been looking for an alternative to this test, because many patients who undergo this invasive procedure end up not even having heart disease. Dr. Warren J. Manning of the Harvard School of Medicine in Boston led an international team to see how well a completely noninvasive procedure called *magnetic-resonance angiography* (MRA) performs in comparison to the invasive coronary angiogram.

They found that the MRA was highly accurate at detecting and ruling out heart disease but that it does have several limitations. For example, the MRA did not allow the physicians to examine 16 percent of the artery segments that could contain disease. In spite of its limitations, though, physicians believe it will eventually become an acceptable alternative to the invasive X-ray angiogram procedure.

CT Angiography (CTA)

Like the coronary angiogram, this procedure is used to identify narrowing of the arteries due to atherosclerosis. It combines a computerized tomography (CT) scan with angiography. (That is, the CT scan is performed after an injection of contrast medium.)

CTAs, however, do not require cardiac catheterization, which makes them a less-invasive procedure than the coronary angiogram. Like the EBCT mentioned on page 61, a CTA also makes an image of calcium deposits.

Many researchers consider the CTA to be an excellent diagnostic tool. The American College of Radiology and the Radiological Society of North America say that it "displays the anatomical detail of blood vessels more precisely than magnetic-resonance imaging (MRI) or ultrasound."

In spite all of these accolades, however, CTA images may turn out fuzzy if the patient moves during the exam or if the heart is not functioning normally. Like the MRI, the procedure cannot be used to reliably produce images of small twisted arteries or vessels in organs that move rapidly.

Treating the Problem

The imaging procedures I have discussed here can help physicians diagnose heart-related problems and make decisions about treatment. The treatment decided upon might include drug therapy and/or another more invasive procedure.

There are many powerful medications that may be prescribed to treat the symptoms of heart disease. Some lower blood-pressure readings, and some slow down the build-up of plaque. Still others can relieve angina attacks.

In addition to drug therapies, there are procedures that fall into a category known as **transcatheter intervention**, which include atherectomies, balloon and laser angioplasties, and stent placements. These require cardiac catheterization and an injection of contrast medium. There also are the fully invasive **surgical procedures**, such as coronary-artery-bypass-graft (CABG) surgery, implantable defibrillators and pacemakers, and heart transplants.

Which of the above a doctor will recommend depends upon an individual's specific situation. He will ask himself a number of

CONTINUED ON PAGE 70

THE FDA'S TIPS FOR TAKING MEDICINES

How to Get the Benefits and Lower the Risks

Whether obtained by prescription or over the counter (OTC), no medicine is without risk. Besides providing benefits, medicines may cause side effects or allergic reactions, and they may be affected by interactions with foods, drinks, or other drugs.

For prescription drugs, a patient's first step to safe and effective treatment is to ask the doctor questions with each new prescription. Here are some examples.

- "What is the medicine's name?" "What is it supposed to do?"
- "How and when do I take it, and for how long?"
- "While taking this medicine, are there any things (certain foods or dietary supplements; caffeine, alcohol, or other beverages; other medicines, prescription or over-the-counter [OTC]; or certain activities, such as driving or smoking) that I should avoid?"
- "Will this new medicine work safely with prescription and OTC medicines I'm already taking?"
- "Are there side effects, and what do I do if they occur?"
- "Will the medicine affect my sleep or activity level?"
- "What should I do if I miss a dose?"
- "Where can I find written information about the medicine?" (At the very least, ask the doctor or pharmacist to write out explicit directions and to provide the technical name for any medicines prescribed.)

It's wise to write down the answers to these questions immediately to make sure you'll remember all the details.

Don't be afraid to ask questions. Pharmacist Michael Cohen, president of the Institute for Safe Medication Practices, Warminster, Pennsylvania, says, "If you can't ask questions comfortably, get someone to do it for you. There are patient advocates in the hospital, and relatives or friends on the outside." "And to prevent mix-ups, patients ought to insist that the medicine's purpose be put on the label," Cohen adds.

More Medicine Tips

Here are more tips for helping your medicines work as safely and effectively as possible.

- Keep a record of all your current medicines, including their names and regimens (dosages, times, and other instructions for taking them). Write down any problems you have with the medicine and discuss them with your doctor or pharmacist.

- Using adequate light, read labels carefully before taking any medicines.

- Ask the doctor's or pharmacist's advice before crushing or splitting tablets; some should only be swallowed whole.

- Contact the doctor or pharmacist if new or unexpected symptoms or other problems appear.

- Never stop taking medicine the doctor has told you to finish just because symptoms disappear.

- Ask the doctor periodically to reevaluate long-term treatments.

- If you have questions, talk to your pharmacist or doctor before using an OTC medicine the first time—especially if you use other medicine.

- Carefully read OTC-medicine labels for ingredients, proper usage, directions, warnings, precautions, and expiration dates. Many medicines contain the same ingredients. Be sure you're not taking the same drug in more than one form.

- Discard outdated medicine.

- Store medicine in the original container, where the label identifies it and gives directions.

- Never store medicine in the bathroom. Unless instructed otherwise, keep it away from heat, light, and moisture.

- Never store medicine near a dangerous substance, which could be taken by mistake.

- Never take someone else's medicine.

- Tell your health professional if you are allergic to certain drugs or foods; have diabetes or kidney or liver disease; take other prescription or OTC medicines regularly, follow a special diet or take dietary supplements; or use alcohol or tobacco.

Source: U.S. Food and Drug Administration, FDA Consumer Magazine, November 1995

questions to help make this decision.

- Where is the blocked artery, and how badly is it blocked?
- How many arteries are affected?
- In what location is the narrowing?
- How much heart muscle is at risk?

Researchers and physicians repeat over and over that no matter how successful these procedures are, they will fail if the patient does not also make lifestyle changes, such as, for example, a better diet and more exercise. Taking medications as prescribed before and/or after any procedures affects the long-term success of these procedures as well.

Prescription-drug Therapies

If your doctor has determined that you have a heart problem, chances are high that you will receive one or more prescriptions for medications. Drug treatments are considered the cornerstone of treatment, and they are generally recommended if changes in diet and exercise don't help. Often, drug therapy will resolve the problems or symptoms occurring and the patient won't have to have any surgery.

The drug prescribed depends upon the symptoms being treated. If a person has several overlapping symptoms, several different types of drugs may be prescribed. Taking aspirin, other medications, and/or vitamin and herbal supplements simultaneously should be approached cautiously and, of course, discussed with your doctor.

This is an area of special concern, because minor and not-so-minor interactions and side effects can occur and prompt complications. Although people should always consult their providers before mixing any or all of their medications, a recent study proves the importance of individual responsibility.

Researchers at Georgetown University Medical Center in

Washington, D.C., found that U.S. medical-school curricula include relatively few courses dedicated to recognizing and reporting adverse drug reactions. In a survey of more than 100 program directors, researchers found that 53 percent of the schools did not offer any training in clinical pharmacology or adverse drug reactions to third- and fourth-year medical students. At those schools where training was available, only 8 percent of the rotations were mandatory—and adverse drug reactions were not reviewed during regular conferences in 18 percent of the schools.

Lucky for us, most physicians learn a lot more about drugs and their reactions once they're in the medical trenches. Here are several of the more commonly prescribed ones for heart-related conditions.

Angiotensin-converting enzyme (ACE) inhibitors. There are several reasons a physician may prescribe an ACE inhibitor like captopril. It can, for example, relieve the symptoms of congestive heart failure (CHF) and help lower one's blood pressure. People who have had a heart attack may receive these drugs as well, because some studies have shown that they may prevent further damage to the heart muscle.

The most common side effect reported is a dry, nagging cough. Another concern for some people is that the level of potassium in their blood increases; in that case, no supplements with potassium should be taken. Certain arthritis drugs can make ACE inhibitors less effective, but, on the flip side, ACE inhibitors also can help decrease blood-sugar levels when used simultaneously with oral diabetes medications.

Blood thinners (anticoagulants). Despite their name, these medications do not thin the blood. They do, however, prevent the blood from clotting. For this reason, anticoagulants, which include aspirin and Coumadin (warfarin), reduce the risk of having a heart attack or stroke. They do not, however, break up clots that have already formed.

In general, the major precaution when taking any blood thinner is to watch for signs of bleeding, since it is, after all, an anticlotting drug. When taking warfarin, it's important to avoid the herbal supplement Gingko, because it too has anticlotting properties and certain antibiotics, which may cause dangerous side effects. There are many over-the-counter medicines (as well as prescriptions) that can lower the effectiveness of blood thinners, including aspirin, acetaminophen, ibuprofen, and antacids.

Beta-blockers. To lower a patient's blood pressure, slow down one's heart rate, or smooth an irregular heartbeat, a physician may prescribe one of the numerous beta-blockers on the market. This can, in turn, decrease angina and ease congestive heart failure. Heart-attack patients may receive this drug to prevent future problems, and people are often given a beta-blocker before surgery to prevent atrial fibrillation.

Here's how this drug works. When a person is under physical or emotional stress, the body sends signals (or adrenaline) to the heart to work harder. These drugs "block" the effect these signals have on your heart and reduce the amount of oxygen needed. As a result, the heart doesn't have to work as hard because it needs less blood and oxygen.

The success of beta-blockers may be linked to the specific drug given and when it's first given to a patient, according to a study sponsored by the National Heart, Lung, and Blood Institute (NHLBI) and the Department of Veterans Affairs. In the Beta-Blocker Evaluation of Survival Trial (BEST), researchers found that a beta-blocker called bucindolol did not increase survival for those with moderate to severe heart failure. So, in other words, the sooner someone is started on a beta-blocker, the better the outcome.

"In BEST, there was a trend toward longer survival for study participants treated with bucindolol who had less advanced heart failure," said Dr. Michael Domanski, leader of a clinical-trials scientific-research group at NHLBI. "That and the results of earlier studies show how important it is to treat heart failure early, when beta-blockers can make a real difference in survival."

"It's still unclear why bucindolol had such varied effects among these patients," said Domanski. "More research is needed so we can understand which patients will benefit from which beta-blocker."

Calcium-channel blockers. These drugs are prescribed to control HBP, angina, and arrhythmia. They work by slowing the rate at which calcium passes into the heart muscle and into the vessel walls. By relaxing the smooth muscles around the arteries and widening the vessels, they allow the blood to flow more easily. This can lower one's blood pressure, relieve angina, and slow down the heart rate.

Doctors frequently recommend that people on these drugs stop smoking, because smoking causes a rapid heartbeat. Some studies show that grapefruit juice drunk less than four hours after taking the drug interferes with the body's absorption. In addition, there are many drugs that could decrease the effectiveness of the calcium-channel blocker.

Cholesterol-lowering medicines. When a person has high levels of total cholesterol or low-density lipoprotein (known as the "bad" cholesterol), a physician usually begins by recommending a program of diet and exercise. If that fails (and studies show it usually does, because people don't stick to the diet), the next step is usually a prescription of one of the available cholesterol-lowering medications.

It is widely accepted that lowering the cholesterol levels of people without heart disease *greatly* reduces their risk of ever developing it. In 1998 the results of an Air Force/Texas coronary atherosclerosis prevention study showed that combining a statin drug with a low-fat diet decreased the risk of experiencing a first-time coronary event by 37 percent. Most of us have heard a lot about *statins*, which are among the most widely prescribed drugs in the world. Over 5 million people in the United States alone are currently taking them.

They work by blocking an enzyme, called HMG-CoA reductase, that causes the body to make LDL cholesterol. Statins are often called the "drugs of first choice" for treating elevated LDL cholesterol, because they usually are effective and, at least according to their promoters, have few short-term side effects. A recent study of heart patients, for example, found that one type of statin drug cut the risk of heart attacks by 60 percent.

Statins are also useful for reducing levels of C-reactive protein, a common blood marker for inflammation (discussed in Chapter 1). In a five-year study of more than 472 heart-attack patients, those who received one of the statins had about 38 percent lower levels of C-reactive protein than those who received a placebo. One of the researchers said that this study demonstrated that the long-term use of pravastatin (one statin drug) does much more than lower cholesterol. However, physicians do not routinely measure C-reactive proteins in the blood.

But, as they say, there's no such thing as a free lunch. Yes, statins work—but at what price? They are certainly expensive in dollar terms, and the physical toll these drugs can take on the body must also be considered.

Statins are "new" drugs (10 or so years old), which means the verdict on their long-term effects isn't in yet. More clinical trials are currently under way. And, in spite of their proven value, all is not perfect. Although not advertised widely, statin drugs are associated with significant side effects, including liver toxicity, sexual dysfunction, and peripheral neuropathy. Most recently, they've been associated with rhabdomyolysis (a disorder involving injury to the kidney caused by a toxin build-up in the muscle cells).

Worse-case scenarios. On Aug. 8, 2001, the FDA announced that Bayer's pharmaceutical division had voluntarily withdrawn Baycol (cerivastatin), a brand-name statin, from the market because of reports of "sometimes fatal" rhabdomyolysis. By early 2002, Bayer estimated that at least 100 people had died who were taking Baycol.

A new study shows that statins can also have more subtle effects on the body—ones that can trigger a whole cascade of health problems down the road. In a Finnish study, doctors researched the effects of the statin drug simvastatin (Zocor) and dietary changes on 120 men between the ages of 35 and 64. All of the men had high cholesterol (fasting serum concentrations between 232 and 309) that had previously been untreated.

The men were randomly divided into two equal groups: Those in one group were advised to continue following their usual diets, while those in the other group were advised to follow a Mediterranean-style diet. Specifically, the dietary intervention included keeping saturated-fat intake below 10 percent of total calories; keeping cholesterol intake below 250 mg a day; and increasing the intake of omega-3 fatty acids, fruits, vegetables, and soluble fiber.

Each group was further divided into two subgroups that took either 20 mg of simvastatin each day or a placebo. They followed this protocol for 12 weeks, and then each subgroup "crossed over" to the other treatment. At baseline and at the end of each

12-week treatment period, the researchers assessed each participant's blood pressure, weight, and exercise frequency, as well as blood levels of cholesterol, insulin, and antioxidants.

There's no denying that simvastatin was effective at reducing cholesterol levels. On the average, the drug brought total-cholesterol levels down 20.8 percent. In contrast, dietary intervention alone decreased total cholesterol by only 7.6 percent.

But here's the revealing finding: Simvastatin treatment also INCREASED fasting serum-insulin levels by 13 percent and DECREASED serum concentrations of important antioxidant vitamins by as much as 22 percent. Among participants in the dietary-intervention group, blood tests revealed significantly lower serum levels of critical nutrients like alpha-tocopherol, betacarotene, and coenzyme Q_{10} while they were taking the statin drug, as compared with the period when they took the placebo. At the same time, glucose levels were not affected—suggesting a decrease in insulin sensitivity.

We know that decreased insulin sensitivity leads us down a dangerous road: to insulin resistance, which leads to Type II diabetes, and finally all the disease's associated conditions, such as kidney disease, heart disease, and even blindness. But not getting the antioxidants you need could be equally troubling. We've learned a lot over the past decade about antioxidants' critical role in good health; these nutrients help protect us from atherosclerosis, Alzheimer's disease, and even cancer.

You could argue that statin drugs also protect us by reducing cholesterol levels and reducing the risk of heart disease. But it seems like a case of robbing Peter to pay Paul. OK, so your cholesterol level comes down, but your insulin levels could go up, and your body could be robbed of essential nutrients.

Considering all of that, is the net effect of statins positive, negative, or just a very expensive wash? You have to make that decision for yourself, after weighing the options with your doctor. But consider that there are safe, natural ways to lower your cholesterol WITHOUT running the risk of insulin resistance, nutrient loss, or other dangerous side effects. Although we often forget this, cholesterol is not the be all and end all of heart-disease prevention.

Later, I'll explain how diet, exercise, and natural remedies should be tried before you resort to statins or other possibly dangerous drugs or procedures. You may have to be a little more patient; you may not see results as quickly and dramatically as you might by taking a pill. But in the end, you'll know for sure that you're netting positive results for your heart and for your overall health.

Beyond statins. Although the statins are very effective in lowering LDL levels, *bile-acid sequestrants* (or resins) also are prescribed alone or with statin drugs. *Fibrate* (a fibric-acid derivative) is another drug sometimes given to lower LDL, but it is mainly prescribed to treat high triglyceride levels and raise one's HDL.

Niacin (nicotinic acid, a form of vitamin B) can also be used to lower LDL trigylceride levels and to raise high-density-lipoprotein (HDL) levels. Niacin is a vitamin that can be purchased without prescription, but those who decide on their own to take it should tell their physicians—particularly since there may be potential interactions and side effects. For example, it can raise blood-sugar and uric-acid levels in the body; it may, therefore, harm those who have diabetes, gout, a gallbladder problem, or liver disease.

To avoid these possibilities and other possible side effects (such as flushing, headaches, and stomachaches), many doctors are now recommending a special form of niacin called inositol hexaniacinate (up to 1,000 mg three times a day). Although this does lower cholesterol without the side effects associated with other forms of niacin, fewer clinical studies have been performed as to other possible long-term side effects—so more caution is being exercised. The general advice about niacin, though, is that it should be taken under a doctor's supervision or obtained through foods, such as peanuts, brewer's yeast, fish, and meat.

Digitalis. This derviative from the foxglove plant has been used to treat heart problems for more than 200 years. It is primarily used to treat congestive heart failure (CHF) and atrial arrhythmias.

Digitalis works by binding with certain receptors in the heart to increase and retain the amount of calcium in the heart cells. The build-up causes a stronger heartbeat, which can help people who have CHF. Digitalis also slows the number of electrical signals that travel through the heart and regulates the number of heartbeats.

Be sure to avoid real licorice (not the artificially produced licorice flavor) if you are taking digitalis, because combining the two can result in irregular heart rhythms and even cardiac arrest.

Diuretics. You might know these as "water pills," and they are referred to by that term because they flush extra fluids (mainly mixtures of salt and water) out of the body. Their primary uses include lowering HBP and easing CHF. There are several types of diuretics, including *thiazide*, which, in addition to their function as water pills, also widen the blood vessels. There are also *potassium-sparing diuretics* that do not cause the body to lose potassium as the other types do. *Loop-acting diuretics* force the kidneys to increase urine flow and thus reduce the amount of fluids retained.

Vasodilators. These drugs are used to treat CHF and to control high blood pressure. They accomplish these tasks by relaxing the smooth vessels of the blood vessels, which enables them to expand

and let blood flow more easily. As a result, the heart doesn't have to pump as hard and the reduced workload reduces the chest pain. Vasodilators are often prescribed for people who cannot tolerate the ACE inhibitors.

One of the most commonly prescribed vasodilators is *nitroglcerin (oral nitrate)*. Nitroglcerin was one of the first man-made drugs. (In other words, as is the case with many of our modern drugs, it's not found in nature.) Nitrates are primarily used to relieve an angina attack that is occurring and to prevent attacks from occurring. Over the long term, they reduce the number of attacks.

Nitrates also may be prescribed to manage CHF or may be prescribed after surgical procedures, such as an angioplasty. In spite of their wonder-drug status, be sure you don't go off them abruptly; doing so could prompt withdrawal symptoms.

Surgical Procedures

Sometimes drug therapy is simply not enough, and there's not much choice (at least from the modern scientific perspective) but to move on to more invasive procedures like surgery. There are many variations on the procedures described below. The options will vary depending on the individual's condition.

Atherectomies. For an artherectomy, a catheter is put into an artery and the surgeon uses one of several tools to remove plaque. One tool is a catheter tip that includes a blade-type device to cut away the plaque. The plaque is stored in a small container that is removed when the catheter is withdrawn from the artery.

Another device is the **rotablator**, which is a catheter with a "burr" at its tip. The burr rotates and grinds the plaque into very small particles, which dissolve into the circulatory system. **Laser**

catheters also can be used to vaporize the plaque. Balloon angioplasty and stenting are often performed after an atherectomy.

The chance of serious complications during an atherectomy is small but slightly higher than that of other catheter-based procedures, such as balloon angioplasty (discussed below).

Angioplasties. The *balloon angioplasty* is considered an established and effective therapy for some patients with coronary-artery disease. Its use has tripled since 1987. When performed successfully, particularly when a stent is simultaneously placed in the artery (see page 81 for more information on stents), 90 percent of the procedures achieve the *initial* goal.

For an angioplasty, a catheter is inserted into an artery through a small skin incision and threaded along the inside of the vessel to the area of the blocked artery. A tiny sausage-shaped balloon filled with fluid is located at the end of the catheter. The balloon is inflated for several seconds to compress the plaque against the artery wall and then deflated. This procedure is repeated several times, with the pressure of the balloon being increased each time. The goal is to enlarge the inner diameter (or lumen) of the artery to allow blood to flow more easily.

A balloon angioplasty, however, has certain limits. It cannot compress arterial blockages that have hardened, nor can it always clear total occlusions. That's where *laser angioplasty* comes in. The catheter used in this method has a laser at its tip. When the laser is in position, it emits pulsating beams of light that burn away the blood clots and plaque that then dissolve into the bloodstream. This procedure can be performed alone or with a balloon angioplasty.

There's also a new type of angioplasty in the halls of medical research that's showing promise. It's called a *cryoplasty*. Pressurized liquid nitrous oxide ("laughing gas") is injected into the balloon after it's inserted. The liquid expands, turns into a gas, and causes the balloon to cool to below zero. The cooling gets rid of the blockage but is gentler on the surrounding tissue than the standard balloon angioplasty.

Trouble in Paradise. In spite of the effectiveness cited with angioplasties, the widened artery often narrows again within six months. This happens in 10 percent to 40 percent of the patients who've had angioplasties. Although another angioplasty might be a possibility, many individuals, at their physician's recommendation, choose to move on to the *coronary-artery-bypass graft (CABG)*.

According to the Nov. 5, 2001, issue of *Circulation: Journal of the American Heart Association*, researchers discovered that more than half of all patients whose heart arteries renarrowed had no symptoms of their renewed disease. What this means is that they could have a silent risk of future heart attacks, according to lead author Dr. Peter N. Ruygrok, consultant cardiologist at Green Lane Hospital in Auckland, New Zealand. "Yet, they believe they have had a successful treatment for their obstructive artery narrowing," he says.

Aside from this, other complications from angioplasties are "unusual," according to the AHA, and an angioplasty is "a less-traumatic and less-expensive alternative to bypass surgery." In a very small percentage of patients, the procedure will not open the artery and CABG surgery will be needed. However, this percentage falls even more when a stent is used.

More than 1 million balloon angioplasties were performed in the United States in 1999. Of the total performed, about 70 percent to 90 percent were followed by the *stent-placement procedure.*

The stent-placement procedure. Since the early 1990s, physicians have been using stents—tiny, meshlike metal scaffolds—after angioplasty to keep an artery open. Restenosis (narrowing or closing of an artery) rates are generally around 15 percent to 20 percent when a stent is in place.

Getting the stent into the artery requires cardiac catheterization and an injection of contrast medium. The stent is mounted on a balloon-tipped catheter, threaded through an artery, and positioned at the site where the artery has been narrowed by plaque. The balloon is then inflated, which opens the stent. The catheter and the deflated balloon are removed, but the stent stays in place permanently. Eventually, the lining of the artery covers the metallic stent.

As stated above, stent placement decreases the odds that restenosis will occur. However, new plaque can grow around the metal to clog the opening again with what some call "remarkable speed." When stents are coated with certain drugs, however, the plaque seems to have a harder time forming.

Dr. Al Raizner, medical director of the Methodist DeBakey Heart Center in Houston, said drug-coated stents are "spectacular developments." According to Raizner, restenosis is "probably the single most important shortcoming in angioplasty today."

The coronary-artery-bypass graft (CABG). For more than 35 years, people with serious heart disease have been having bypass surgery; it is now one of the most frequently performed surgeries in the country. A 1998 report from the American College of Cardiology called CABG "one of the greatest success stories in medicine." More than half a million CABGs were performed in 1999.

A CABG reroutes blood around clogged arteries so that blood flow resumes. In this procedure, an incision is made in the middle of the chest, the breastbone is separated, and the ribs are spread apart. The surgeon takes a blood vessel from another part of the body and creates a graft (or blood vessel) to use to restore blood flow. In the traditional surgery, a patient's heart will be stopped, and a heart-lung machine will resume cardiovascular functions. (There's also the "off-pump" technique, which may be used.) The graft is attached above and below the area in the vessel where the blockage is located. The blood uses the new, unblocked pathway.

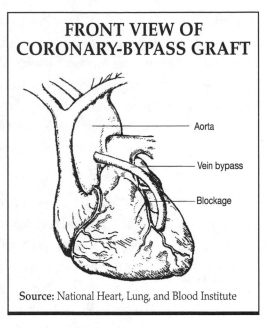

FRONT VIEW OF CORONARY-BYPASS GRAFT

Aorta

Vein bypass

Blockage

Source: National Heart, Lung, and Blood Institute

Generally, vessels remain open for 10 years or more. However, a CABG is not a sure thing either. Although it does improve blood flow, it doesn't prevent blockage from reoccurring, and, of course, not everyone who has coronary heart disease needs this surgery. Once again, many people can improve their odds with a better diet and more exercise. Others may need more medication, angioplasty, and other nonsurgical procedures.

Research lists several possible risks of the procedure, but the chances of their occurring are low. Between 95 percent and 98 percent of such procedures are said to have "no serious complications." However, statistics from the National Institutes of Health say that heart attacks occur during about 5 percent of bypasses performed. The risk of stroke for people over 70 is 5 percent to 10 percent. In general, the risks increase for the elderly, for people with damaged hearts or diabetes, and for those who have had other heart operations.

Defibrillators. These devices come in several different styles, but they all have the job of monitoring and correcting tachycardia (a rapid heartbeat). Most of us know defibrillators best through the medical shows we see on television. When we see the electronic "paddles" pulled out of a corner of the emergency room and hear the technician shout "clear," we're seeing a manual defibrillator in action. More and more laypeople, such as fire and police personnel, are being trained to use *automatic external defibrillators* to shock the heart back into rhythm.

The defibrillator that requires surgery for its use is called an **implantable cardioverter defibrillator (ICD)**. The ICD is programmed and surgically implanted into a person's chest. It runs on batteries, but there's no reason to worry if you or a loved one gets one, because they generally last for more than five years, and they don't run out unexpectedly. A built-in warning is activated when batteries run low, and your physician will monitor your defibrillator's strength on a regular basis and replace it when necessary. Many ICDs are wallet-sized, but the latest versions are tiny enough to be inserted through a blood vessel.

For people who experience ventricular tachycardia (a rapid heartbeat), the ICD will stimulate the heart to restore normal rhythm. For those with ventricular fibrillation (a quivering, but not beating, heart), the ICD will deliver an electric shock. The goal is to get the heartbeat back to normal rhythm immediately and avoid sudden cardiac arrest.

According to the AHA, ICDs have been "very useful in preventing sudden death in patients with known, sustained ventricular tachycardia or fibrillation." They aren't always perfect, however, and the number of advisories about implanted heart devices from the Food and Drug Administration (FDA) has been increasing. (See page 85 under the heading "Pacemakers.")

Pacemakers. As stated in Chapter 2, the heart does have its own natural pacemaker (the sinoatrial node). In this chapter, however, we're talking about an artificial, electronic one that's implanted in the chest to regulate the heart's rhythm. Like the ICDs, pacemakers restore normal rhythm to the heartbeat. But unlike ICDs, pacemakers focus on *bradycardia* (slow heartbeats).

The procedure for inserting a battery-powered pacemaker varies depending on whether an external temporary device or an internal, permanent one will be used. As you might expect, insertion of a temporary pacemaker is less invasive than insertion of a permanent device. A surgical procedure is required to insert the pacemaker inside the chest (or abdomen). The general assertion is that pacemakers significantly improve people's lives and that most recipients resume normal activities.

However, certain environments may interfere with pacemaker functioning. For example, people who have them must avoid any areas that contain equipment that generates strong electrical or magnetic fields, such as magnetic-resonance-imaging machines and metal detectors. The FDA recommends that people with pacemakers avoid leaning against or lingering near store security gates as well.

Cellular phones rarely cause interference with pacemakers *except* when they are placed directly over the implantation site. The risk of interference is greater with digital cell phones and dual-chamber pacemakers. The solution is simple: Hold the phone at least 6 inches from the pacemaker generators, even when the phone's turned off.

FDA advisories. One word of caution was recently published in medical literature regarding the incidence of a *staph* infection within six years of insertion of a pacemaker. In most of the cases, the source of the infection was the implanted device itself. Although this study was small, researchers say that about 20 percent of patients with implanted pacemakers develop this problem. They recommend that physicians replace the device rather than trying to treat the infection.

Another concern is the fact that recalls and safety alerts for implanted heart devices increased between 1990 and 2000. (Note also that the number of devices implanted increased 49 percent.) During those 10 years, the FDA issued advisories affecting 400,000 pacemakers and 114,000 ICDs. Although more pacemakers were affected, the ICDs had a higher recall rate.

Advisories may lead to device checks and/or future recalls, and the increasing number of these underscores the need for patients to memorize the make and model numbers of their pacemakers and defibrillators and to carry their device-information cards. By doing so, they can determine quickly if an advisory concerns their implanted devices.

Heart transplants. Open-heart surgery was first performed in 1967. Its goal is to replace a severely diseased or damaged heart with a healthy heart from a recently deceased person. About 80 percent of heart-transplant patients survive for one year or longer after the procedure, and 50 percent live nine years or more.

There is, unfortunately, a very large roadblock to getting a heart transplant. The number of people waiting for a healthy heart is significantly higher than the number of hearts available. Specifically, according to the United Network for Organ Sharing, more than 40,000 people were on the waiting list as of February 2000. Compare that figure to the fact that only 2,345 received a donated heart in 1998.

This "waiting game" is considered the hardest part of the

transplant process. People waiting for a healthy heart are encouraged to focus on emotional, medical, and lifestyle changes and to continue medical therapies that provide short-term relief of their heart conditions.

This is, of course, a very high-risk procedure with two risks topping the list. First, the body may reject the new heart because it perceives it as a foreign "invader" that it must fight. To reduce the immune system's power to destroy the new heart, immunosuppressant drugs are given. However, these medications can weaken the body's ability to fight infection and rejection can still occur.

The future of heart transplants may be brighter, however, for those waiting on human hearts. Some researchers are trying to find ways of prolonging the patient's life until the right match can be found, while others are hoping that a totally artificial heart may be used as a permanent solution. Then there's the longer-term goal of a genetically engineered heart. This would involve creating a new organ from human tissues that are grown over several months. Currently, this "heart in a box" project exists only in research facilities.

Getting Back to TLC

I'm guessing that you've probably heard enough by now about the wonders of modern medicine. As far as I'm concerned, the information in this chapter is enough to inspire most people to look long and hard at the alternatives for lowering the risk factors for heart disease. Making some therapeutic lifestyle changes (TLCs) seems pretty easy now, doesn't it?

In the next few chapters, you'll find the TLCs you need to help your heart; we'll start with the right kind of diet.

CHAPTER 4

Dietary Interventions for a Healthy Heart

For more than half of us, the most successful prescription for a healthy heart doesn't come in the shape of a pill. It simply involves eating low-fat, low-cholesterol foods. As you've discovered by reading the previous chapters, atherosclerosis (hardening or narrowing of the arteries that supply blood to the heart) leads to most heart problems, including high blood pressure, angina, and heart attacks.

The formula for dietary intervention and a healthier heart is a simple one. However, as most of us know, it's one thing to understand this concept and quite another to make the changes needed to make it a reality. But strides toward that goal, however small, will help.

The most sensible starting point on your path to a healthy heart is to adopt a *balanced diet* that provides the body with the nutrients needed to keep it running efficiently. Such a diet also helps to fill you up and, at least in theory, decrease the foods that contribute to heart disease.

As you'll see as you go through this chapter and the next one, there are many kinds of foods, vitamins, and herbs that help the heart. It's practically impossible to single out the best ones, which is why starting out with a balanced diet makes so much sense.

Dietary Guidelines

In 2000, the government released a revision of its *Dietary Guidelines for Americans*. This publication—an initiative developed by the U.S. Department of Health and Human Services and the Department of Agriculture—includes the food-guide pyramid that most of you will recognize, shown on page 91. The *dietary guidelines* have become the "gold standard" for applying scientific research to what people should be eating. Most heart experts consider this pyramid to be a good starting point (although it may not be perfect for everyone).

This latest version of the guidelines also emphasizes the importance of regular exercise (discussed in Chapter 6) and proper preparation of foods in the kitchen. Food preparation was included because improper handling of food can increase the chance of certain food-borne illnesses. For example, though rare, pathogens like *Salmonella*, *Clostridium*, and *Staphylococcus* can enter the bloodstream and have been linked to heart conditions like congestive heart failure.

Extensive research has been done on the basic concepts illustrated by the food-guide pyramid. Think of this as the *first* step toward a healthier heart.

Getting Down to Basics

If you take a look at the food-guide pyramid, you will see that fats, oils, and sweets (at the top) should be eaten "sparingly." These are the foods that most of us love to overindulge in, so consuming them sparingly may be a challenge. This challenge brings to mind the phrase I mentioned in Chapter 1—"therapeutic lifestyle change" (TLC). The National Cholesterol Education Program (NCEP) coined this phrase, which involves three parts: a cholesterol-lowering diet (the TLC diet), physical activity, and weight management.

A healthy heart certainly requires these changes, and it also requires another kind of TLC—tender loving care. At first, a lot of TLC—and patience—may be required to get, and stay, on the right track. Don't despair if you fall off the track; just get right back on, and keep on trying!

Notice that foods with the most nutrients and the least fats—grains, vegetables, and fruits—form the foundation of the pyramid. These foods, as well as beans, are low in fats, sodium, and cholesterol, and increasing your use of them is just as important as reducing your intake of fats, oils, and sweets. Filling up on the foods at the bottom of the pyramid can help you fight cholesterol—and the resulting atherosclerosis.

Since the government developed this food-guide pyramid in 1992, several variations have been introduced that take into account other preferred food choices. Now, there are pyramids for Latin, Asian, Mediterranean, and vegetarian cooking. The American Diabetes Association has even developed a diabetic food-guide pyramid, which includes several substantial changes to the traditional pyramid.

Some experts believe that the closer to a vegetarian diet people at risk for heart disease can come, the better their hearts will be. By comparing the vegetarian-diet pyramid (page 92) with the standard food-guide pyramid, you can see what changes are required to adopt a vegetarian diet.

Lose Weight

Adopting these basic rules and others discussed below can

CONTINUED ON PAGE 92

FOOD-GUIDE PYRAMID
A Guide to Daily Food Choices

Fats, Oils, & Sweets
USE SPARINGLY

KEY
● Fat (naturally occurring and added)
▼ Sugars (added)
These symbols show fat and added sugars in foods.

Milk, Yogurt, & Cheese Group
2-3 SERVINGS

Meat, Poultry, Fish, Dry Beans, Eggs, & Nuts Group
2-3 SERVINGS

Vegetable Group
3-5 SERVINGS

Fruit Group
2-4 SERVINGS

Bread, Cereal, Rice, & Pasta Group
6-11 SERVINGS

Source: U.S. Department of Agriculture/U.S. Department of Health and Human Services

WHAT COUNTS AS A SERVING?

Bread, Cereal, Rice, and Pasta Group (Grains Group)—whole grain and refined
- 1 slice of bread
- About 1 cup of ready-to-eat cereal
- 1/2 cup of cooked cereal, rice, or pasta

Vegetable Group
- 1 cup of raw leafy vegetables
- 1/2 cup of other vegetables—cooked or raw
- 3/4 cup of vegetable juice

Fruit Group
- 1 medium apple, banana, orange, pear
- 1/2 cup of chopped, cooked, or canned fruit
- 3/4 cup of fruit juice

Milk, Yogurt, and Cheese Group (Milk Group)*
- 1 cup of milk** or yogurt**
- 1 1/2 ounces of natural cheese** (such as cheddar)
- 2 ounces of processed cheese** (such as American)

Meat, Poultry, Fish, Dry Beans, Eggs, and Nuts Group (Meat and Beans Group)
- 2–3 ounces of cooked lean meat, poultry, or fish
- 1/2 cup of cooked dry beans or 1/2 cup of tofu counts as 1 ounce of lean meat
- 2 1/2-ounce soyburger or 1 egg counts as 1 ounce of lean meat
- 2 tablespoons of peanut butter or 1/3 cup of nuts counts as 1 ounce of meat

* This includes lactose-free and lactose-reduced milk products. One cup of soy-based beverage with added calcium is an option for those who prefer a non-dairy source of calcium.

** Choose fat-free or reduced-fat dairy products most often.

Dry beans, peas, and lentils can be counted as servings in either the meat and beans group or the vegetable group. As a vegetable, 1/2 cup of cooked, dry beans counts as 1 serving. As a meat substitute, 1 cup of cooked, dry beans counts as 1 serving (2 ounces of meat).

NOTE: Many of the serving sizes given above are smaller than those on the Nutrition Facts Label. For example, 1 serving of cooked cereal, rice, or pasta is 1 cup for the label but only 1/2 cup for the Pyramid.

help tackle problems with excess weight—a major risk factor for heart disease. People who are overweight are already at greater risk for high blood pressure, high blood cholesterol or other lipid disorders, Type-2 diabetes, heart disease, a stroke, and certain cancers. An overweight body has to work harder to keep low-density-lipoprotein cholesterol (the bad one) under control and increase the healthy, high-density-lipoprotein cholesterol.

According to the findings of one study, published in early 2002, people who are overweight have higher incidences of inflammation in the body. As you'll remember from Chapter 1, inflammation, which is the body's reaction to infection, contributes to clogged arteries. Up until this study, researchers couldn't put a finger on what caused inflammation but being overweight may be

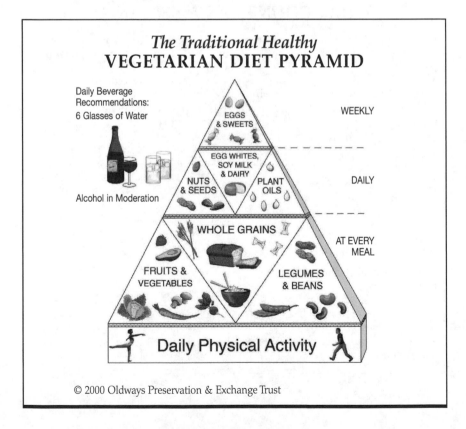

The Traditional Healthy
VEGETARIAN DIET PYRAMID

Daily Beverage Recommendations:
6 Glasses of Water

EGGS & SWEETS

WEEKLY

EGG WHITES, SOY MILK & DAIRY

NUTS & SEEDS

PLANT OILS

DAILY

Alcohol in Moderation

WHOLE GRAINS

AT EVERY MEAL

FRUITS & VEGETABLES

LEGUMES & BEANS

Daily Physical Activity

© 2000 Oldways Preservation & Exchange Trust

one contributing factor.

Researchers from the department of medicine at the University of Vermont, Burlington looked at 61 overweight women with an average age of 56. They measured levels of C-reactive protein (CRP) in their blood. (Remember from Chapter 2 that when inflammation in the body rises, this substance increases.) The researchers then put these women on a weight-loss program. On the average, CRP levels dropped by 32 percent after the women lost an average of 33 pounds over 14 months. The more fat the women lost, the more the CRP fell.

The message is simple. Whether you're a woman or a man, even a small weight loss (just 10 percent of your current weight) will help lower your risks of heart disease.

Good Fats, Bad Fats

Fats do *many* good things for us, such as supply energy and help us absorb several fat-soluble vitamins (A, D, E, and K). We all need to eat *some* fat, but research shows that most of us go way overboard. In fact, according to some estimates, Americans get an average of 34 percent of their calories from total fat (about 12 percent from saturated fat, the worst kind for the heart).

Eating more fat than our bodies need for energy can lead to weight gain and contribute to coronary artery disease. The *major* goal of a heart-healthy diet is to enable you to consume less saturated fat and dietary cholesterol. This means cutting *way* down on any foods that come from animals.

There are several types of fats, but three types, because they cause the liver to produce more cholesterol, definitely belong on the "use sparingly" list.

S O U R C E S O F T H E " B A D " F A T S	
Type of Fat	**Where You'll Find It**
saturated	whole-milk dairy products (including cheese and ice cream); fatty and processed meat; poultry (especially the skin); and tropical oils, such as palm and coconut oils
trans fatty acids	any food high in partially hydrogenated vegetable oils (hard margarine and shortening), including cookies, crackers, chips, fried foods (especially French fries), and bakery goods like doughnuts. (Think "junk food.")
dietary cholesterol	liver and other organ meats, egg yolks, and dairy products made with whole milk

Saturated fats. These fats, the most dangerous of them all, come mainly from animal products and some plant oils. Foods that include saturated fats, such as meat and whole-milk products, raise the levels of LDL cholesterol and triglycerides in the blood. Many prepackaged foods claim to contain "low cholesterol" or "no cholesterol." Although this may be true, they still could be high in saturated fats. This fact is an important one, which involves reading the information on nutrition labels—a habit you'll need to adopt, by the way!

Trans fatty acids. These fats are produced through a manufacturing process called *hydrogenation*, which makes unsaturated fats (the good fats) behave like saturated fats. Vegetable oils, for example, are modified or processed to create solids (such as margarine). Products that include trans fats (or partially hydrogenated vegetable oils) can be found in many commercial baked goods and fast foods. All of these "comfort" foods can raise total and LDL cholesterol and lower HDL cholesterol.

A recent Harvard University study of more than 80,000 women suggested that replacing just 2 percent of calories from trans fatty acids with unsaturated fats reduces the risk of heart disease by more than 50 percent.

Dietary cholesterol. Although saturated and trans fats are the two main culprits in heart disease, foods high in dietary cholesterol also raise the level of blood cholesterol. They come from animal foods, particularly organ meats (like liver), egg yolks, whole-milk dairy products, fish, and poultry.

It can get complicated trying to figure out which of the fat-laden foods are worse than the others. Sometimes comparisons, such as in the following example, can help clarify that choice. A single large-egg yolk has about 250 mg of cholesterol. Three ounces of chicken have about 65 mg of cholesterol. If you were trying to stay under the American Heart Association's recommended cholesterol intake per day (which is between 200 mg and 300 mg), which one would you choose? Remember, of course, that the egg isn't the only thing you'd be eating that day.

Tune Into the "Good" Fats

Not all fats are created equal, however. **Unsaturated fats,** which are found mainly in plant and nut oils, do not increase our cholesterol or triglyceride levels, and some may even help to reduce them. *Polyunsaturated fats,* for example, help the body get rid of newly formed cholesterol. *Monounsaturated fats* also may help reduce cholesterol, as long as your diet is low in saturated fat.

One type of monounsaturated fat that has received a lot of

attention is *olive oil*, which has been found to lower LDL cholesterol when it replaces saturated fat in the diet. One study, the results of which were published in a 1999 issue of the *American Journal of Clinical Nutrition*, found that high amounts of olive oil in the diet can lower the risk of cardiovascular disease by 25 percent, as compared with a 12 percent decrease for a low-fat diet.

Another positive form of fat is *Omega-3 essential fatty acid*, which comes from cold-water fish (like salmon, sardines, bluefish, and tuna). The consumption of these fish is proving to be quite valuable in combating many medical conditions, including heart-related ones. Numerous studies have shown that eating this type of fish two or three times a week offers many health benefits. It can help lower levels of triglycerides in the blood and platelet aggregation, slow the accumulation of atherosclerosis in the blood vessels, and reduce arrhythmias. There are even studies that say omega-3s are beneficial because they modulate the heart's electrical activity.

A study published in the *Journal of Cardiology* found that individuals with high levels of a certain type of omega-3 fatty acid in their cells had lower levels of CRP in their blood. Researchers believe that the fatty acid inhibited the formation of CRP, which is found in high levels in cases of blood-vessel inflammation (which, in turn, appears to contribute to plaque build-up). Other studies also have shown links between high blood levels of CRP and an increased heart-attack risk in otherwise healthy people.

However, a slight variation on these findings was uncovered in a follow-up study conducted by the Harvard Health Professionals. These researchers concluded that fish consumption doesn't reduce the risk of heart disease but may reduce the risk of dying from it. Another study (the results of which were published in 1997) followed 1,800 men for 30 years and found that those who ate at least

8 ounces of fish a week had a 40 percent lower risk of a fatal heart attack than those who ate no fish. (Fish oil can also be taken as a supplement, and I've discussed that in Chapter 5.)

Flaxseed oil is another item in the unsaturated-fat category that may help lower cholesterol and high blood pressure. Like most vegetable oils, it contains *linoleic acid;* however, it also has the added benefit of containing *alpha-linoloenic acid* (ALA). (In fact, flaxseed and the oil made from it are the best food sources for ALA.) Flaxseed oil is rich in omega-3 (from the ALA) and omega-6 (from the linoleic acid) fatty acids. In regard to omega-3, it's been said to contain more than twice as much as fish oils! What's more, it's a rich source of dietary fiber. It's even thought to provide more protection than olive oil does. Try a tablespoon or two of *flaxseed oil* on a salad or vegetables every day. Note that this oil isn't good for cooking, because the heat destroys its heart-rich benefits.

Many studies are now finding that *nuts* may actually benefit the heart. Researchers from the Harvard School of Public Health studied more than 86,000 women and discovered that those who ate at least 5 ounces of nuts a week cut their risk of heart disease

---

S O U R C E S   O F   T H E   " B E T T E R "   F A T

Type of Fat	Where You'll Find Them
unsaturated fat *(monounsaturated, polyunsaturated, and omega-3 fatty acids)*	*polyunsaturated fats:* safflower oil, sesame, soy, corn and sunflower-seed oils, nuts, and seeds. *monounsaturated fats:* olive, canola, and peanut oils plus avocados. *Omega-3 fatty acid* (a type of monounsaturated fat): cold-water fish like salmon and tuna

by a third! Preliminary results in men showed similar benefits.

It turns out that nuts are high in unsaturated fats, alpha-linolenic acid, and other nutrients, particularly hard-to-get minerals like copper, magnesium, and zinc. On top of that, they're full of arginine, fiber, folic acid, and potassium. Calcium is also found in high amounts in nuts. An ounce of almonds, for example, provides 80 mg of calcium, which is about 8 percent of the amount we need every day. Walnuts, though, seem to be at the top of the heart-healthy list, because they contain the highest amount of ALA.

In spite of the more positive nature of unsaturated fats, always remember that they are *still* fat and should be eaten in moderation. As a general guideline, check that your total daily fat intake is no more than 30 percent of your total calories. Saturated fats should be less than 10 percent of total calories. See the box below for guidelines on fat consumption.

THE UPPER LIMIT ON FAT CONSUMPTION

Total Calories per Day	Saturated Fat in Grams	Total Fat in Grams
1,200	13	40
1,500	17	50
1,800	20	60
2,000	22	67
2,200	24	73
2,500	28	83
3,000	33	100

Source: American Heart Association

The AHA Weighs in on Diet

The American Heart Association and the National Cholesterol Education Program developed a program made up of what the organizations refer to as their step-I and step-II diets to lower LDL cholesterol. Like other generally accepted heart-healthy diets, they focus on reducing saturated fat and cholesterol while promoting good nutrition.

The step-I diet is recommended for people at *risk* of cardiovascular disease (CVD), not for people with identified heart problems. The AHA recommends that people with high cholesterol levels (240 mg/dL and higher) or those who have had a heart attack start with the step-II goals. These changes should be combined with regular physical activity. Also, if you are overweight you should aim to lose the extra pounds.

RECOMMENDED INTAKE OF FAT AND CHOLESTEROL
AS A PERCENTAGE OF TOTAL CALORIES

Nutrient*	Step-I Diet	Step-II Diet
total fat	30% or less	30% or less
saturated fat	7% to 10%	Less than 7%
polyunsaturated fat	Up to 10%	Up to 10%
monounsaturated fat	Up to 15%	Up to 15%
cholesterol	Less than 300 mg per day	Less than 200 mg per day

* *Calories from alcohol are not included.*

Source: American Heart Association

A translation of these percentages into calories goes like this: If you consume 2,000 calories a day, your goal would be to consume 30 percent or less of those calories in total fat grams. That equals about 67 total grams of fat per day. The AHA translated the percentages for the public, shown in the table below.

RECOMMENDED AMOUNTS OF TOTAL FAT AND SATURATED FAT IN GRAMS			
Calorie Level	Total Fat (grams)	Step-I Diet Saturated Fat (grams)	Step-II Diet Saturated Fat (grams)
1,200	40 or less	9 to 13	Less than 9
1,500	50 or less	12 to 17	Less than 12
1,800	60 or less	14 to 20	Less than 14
2,000	67 or less	16 to 22	Less than 16
2,200	73 or less	17 to 24	Less than 17
2,500	83 or less	19 to 28	Less than 19
3,000	100 or less	23 to 33	Less than 23

Source: American Heart Association

Tips for Fighting Fat and Cholesterol

If you put your mind to it, it's not really that hard to decrease the amounts of saturated fat and cholesterol in your diet. Here are some tips that will help:

- Eat a variety of fruits and vegetables (at least five servings) and of beans and grains (at least six servings). Fill half of your plate with these foods and eat them first before tackling the other foods on the plate. Doing so may help reduce the amount you consume.

- Choose vegetable oils (such as corn and olive oils) over butter for cooking, or, even better, use nonfat cooking sprays.

- Use olive oil, vinegar, and herbs to dress salads instead of using other fat-filled dressings.

- Eat more seafood and lean poultry than high-fat, high-cholesterol meat (such as bacon, sausage, bologna, salami, etc.). When you do eat meat and poultry, remove as much fat as possible. Broil or roast it instead of frying it. Avoid organ meats, such as liver.

- Avoid convenience foods, as well as commercial baked goods.

- Switch to low-fat dairy products (like skim milk and nonfat yogurt).

- Use mustard instead of mayonnaise and other fatty spreads on sandwiches.

- Reduce or eliminate whole eggs from your diet. Egg whites can be used instead.

- Use nonfat yogurt instead of sour cream for recipes and part-skim ricotta cheese in recipes that call for cream cheese.

- Choose and prepare foods with less salt.

- Drink alcohol in moderation if you drink at all.

- Limit foods and beverages that contain a high sugar content.

Hold the Salt

It is the job of salt (*sodium chloride*) to regulate the fluid balance of cells and plasma in the body. When we get too little salt, we get dehydrated; that's because our cells can't retain water. Too much salt can increase our risk of high blood pressure. Overweight people who eat too much salt raise their risk of having a stroke. At present, the firmest link between salt intake and health relates to blood pressure. People who already have HBP raise their risk of kidney damage.

Although the body of the average person needs only about half a gram of salt per day, the average American consumes between 9 grams and 12 grams of salt per day. About a teaspoon of salt per day, or about 2,400 mg (or 2.4 grams), is more than enough. Most of us get enough through the naturally occurring sodium found in fruits and vegetables.

There is new information concerning the connection between salt and hypertension coming to light every day. There is **not** a definitive connection between salt intake and high blood pressure. However, there is certainly a suggested relationship—at least in people who are salt-sensitive or who already have had problems with high blood pressure. Eating salt does **not** cause high blood pressure; it most accurately would be categorized as a risk factor, meaning that it raises your *risk* of developing HBP. Since it is clear that the U.S. diet is entirely too high in salt and that there are a number of additional health problems associated with a diet high in salt, most experts agree it is a good idea to cut back on our salt intake.

Although keeping salt to a minimum may be achievable when you cook your own foods, it is more of a challenge when you eat in restaurants or eat processed and prepared foods (such as those that are frozen, canned, or otherwise prepackaged). Salt is also used as a natural preservative for meats and vegetables. But there are ways to reduce salt intake, and one place to start is by reading the nutrition labels affixed to products.

Phrase	What It Means (sodium per serving)
sodium-free	5 mg or less
very-low sodium	35 mg or less
low sodium	140 mg or less
reduced or less sodium	At least 25 percent less sodium than the regular version
light in sodium	50 percent less sodium than the regular version
salt-free	5 mg or less
low-sodium meal	140 mg per 100 grams

DASH Helps

For a long time, researchers were trying to find clues about what dietary items affect blood pressure by testing various single nutrients, such as calcium and magnesium. These studies were done mostly with dietary supplements, and their findings were not conclusive. Then, scientists supported by the National Heart, Lung, and Blood Institute (NHLBI) conducted two key studies.

In the first study, called "DASH," short for dietary approaches to stop hypertension, researchers tested nutrients as they occur together in food. They found that blood pressure could be reduced via an eating plan that is low in saturated fat, cholesterol, and total fat and high in fruits, vegetables, and low-fat dairy foods. This eating plan—now known as the DASH diet—also includes a lot of whole-grain products, fish, poultry, and nuts but does not include much red meat or sweets, particularly sugar-containing beverages. It is rich in magnesium, potassium, and calcium, as well as protein and fiber.

DASH research involved 459 adults. About 27 percent had high blood pressure. The research compared three eating plans: one similar in nutrients to what many Americans consume, another much like the first one but higher in fruits and vegetables, and the DASH diet. All three came in at about 3,000 mg of sodium daily. None of the plans was a vegetarian diet or included specialty foods.

According to the NHLBI, results were dramatic: Both the fruits-and-vegetables plan and the DASH diet reduced blood pressure. But the DASH diet had the greatest effect, especially for those with high blood pressure. Furthermore, the blood-pressure reductions came fast—within two weeks of the time the plan was started.

Guidelines of the DASH diet might sound familiar.

- Reduce the overall amount of fat, particularly saturated fat, you consume and reduce sweets and sugar-containing drinks.

- Increase the number of fruits, vegetables, and low-fat dairy foods in your diet.

- Moderately restrict your salt and calorie intake.

By following the DASH plan, people lowered their blood pressure to the same extent as did those people who took antihypertensives (drugs for lowering blood pressure)! Other studies have evaluated the DASH diet and found that it also appears to lower cholesterol and homocysteine levels. According to researchers, widespread use of the DASH diet could reduce the incidence of coronary-artery disease by 15 percent and stroke by 27 percent. In general, it's considered a real benefit for people with or without high blood pressure.

To show you what you will be eating if you adopt the DASH diet, see the sample menu on the next page.

DASH Plus

In late 2001, the NHLBI released the findings of another study—called the DASH-sodium study. Like the original DASH study, this one also evaluated the blood pressure of individuals. Instead of just changing their diets, however, participants reduced their intake of dietary salt *and* followed either the DASH diet or the typical eating plan of most Americans.

Results of the study showed that reducing salt intake lowered blood pressure no matter which eating plan a person was following. Those following the DASH diet while taking in the lowest amount of sodium (1,500 milligrams, the lowest range included in the study), however, had the biggest blood pressure reductions. The largest drop in blood-pressure was observed in those individuals who had pre-existing hypertension, but those without hypertension had significant decreases as well.

The final word is this: A combination of the DASH diet *and* sodium reduction can lower blood pressure for everyone. The NHLBI called the DASH diet *and* lower salt intake a true winning combination.

A SAMPLE MENU FROM THE DASH DIET

The sample menu below provides the following: 2,010 calories, 5 servings of fruits, 7 servings of vegetables, 3 servings of dairy foods, 59 grams of fat, 121 milligrams of cholesterol, and 1,356 milligrams of sodium.

	Amount	Amount of Sodium (in milligrams)
Breakfast:		
cereal, shredded wheat	1/2 cup	2
skim milk	1 cup	126
orange juice	1 cup	5
banana, raw	1 medium	1
bread, 100% whole wheat	1 slice	149
Lunch:		
chicken salad	3/4 cup	151
bread, 100% whole wheat	2 slices	298
dijon mustard	1 teaspoon	125
tomatoes, raw, fresh	2 large slices	6
mixed cooked vegetables	1 cup	25
fruit cocktail, juice pack	1/2 cup	5
Dinner:		
baked cod	3 ounces	93
fresh frozen snap or green beans, cooked without salt	1 cup	11
potato, baked, flesh and skin, w/o salt	1 large	15
sour cream, lowfat	2 tablespoons	30
chives (or scallions)	1 tablespoon	0
fat-free natural cheddar cheese	3 tablespoons	169
tossed salad with mixed greens	1 1/2 cups	25
olive oil and vinegar dressing	2 tablespoons	0
Snack:		
orange juice	1/2 cup	3
almonds, dried, blanched, w/o salt	1/3 cup	3
raisins, seedless	1/4 cup	5
yogurt, blended, fat-free with sugar	1 cup	103

Source: National Heart, Lung, and Blood Institute of the National Institutes of Health

Tips for Reducing Sodium the DASH Way

- Use reduced-sodium or no-salt-added products, such as no-salt-added canned vegetables or dry cereals that have no added salt.

- Be "spicy" instead of "salty" in cooking. Flavor foods with a variety of herbs, spices, wine, lemon, lime, or vinegar. Be creative!

- Avoid the saltshaker on the table, or replace the salt with an herb substitute.

- Eat more whole, unprocessed foods. Decrease your consumption of processed, canned, and convenience foods.

- Avoid such condiments as soy sauce, teriyaki sauce, and monosodium glutamate (MSG), or use the lower-sodium versions.

- Read food labels to become aware of high-sodium foods and to select the varieties lowest in sodium.

- Limit cured foods (such as bacon and ham), foods packed in brine (such as pickles, pickled vegetables, olives, and sauerkraut), and condiments like mustard, horseradish, ketchup, and Worcestershire sauce.

- Modify recipes by doing the following. Reduce the salt in recipes by cutting the amount in half. Use lemon juice, vinegar, and herbs and spices to enhance flavor. Replace salt- and sodium- containing ingredients with lower-sodium alternatives.

- When eating in restaurants:
  - Ask how foods are prepared. Request that

they be prepared without added salt, MSG, or salt-containing ingredients. Most restaurants will be willing to accommodate your request.

♦ Know the terms that indicate high sodium: pickled, soy sauce, in broth, and cured, for example.

♦ Move the saltshaker away.

■ Limit such condiments as mustard, ketchup, pickles, and sauces with salt-containing ingredients.

■ Choose fruits or vegetables instead of salty snack foods.

Fill Up On Fiber

When trying to convince people to cut their intake of saturated fats, heart experts often say to fill up on fiber—**soluble fiber**, that is. This is the type that, when eaten as part of a regular diet, helps lower levels of total and LDL cholesterol in the blood. Examples of soluble fiber include psyllium (a seed husk), whole oats, beans, peas, rice bran, pearl barley, certain fruits (such as oranges, pears, strawberries, and apple pulp), and certain vegetables (such as brussel sprouts and carrots). *Flaxseed* is another source of soluble fiber. Note, if you suffer from thyroid problems please consult your doctor before increasing your intake of flaxseed, soy or walnuts as they are major goitrogens.

Several of the foods in the fiber category claim special status in the cholesterol-lowering realm. For example, some studies have found that psyllium is a must for people with moderately high cholesterol levels. In fact, the Food and Drug Administration (FDA) now allows foods that contain 1.7 grams of psyllium per serving to carry the heart-healthy label usually associated with oatmeal and soy products. (See page 109.)

Researchers from the Veterans Affairs Medical Center and the University of Kentucky analyzed the results of eight studies that evaluated the effects of psyllium on cholesterol levels. On the average, the study participants who took 10 grams of psyllium a day had a drop of 7 percent in their LDL levels. Many of these participants had already lowered their cholesterol by following the AHA diet. According to the researchers, this suggests that combining a fiber supplement of psyllium with a heart-healthy diet shows promise for additional benefits.

Oatmeal is another one of the heart's superstars. Researchers have found that eating oatmeal for 30 days actually *removes* cholesterol from the body. Oats bind with the cholesterol-based acids and prevent them from being absorbed into the bloodstream. If you see the following statement on oat products, such as cereal, you'll know that it passed the FDA's test. "Three grams of soluble fiber from oatmeal daily, in a diet low in saturated fat and cholesterol, may reduce the risk of heart disease."

Bulking up the diet with *legumes* like beans and peas also can lower the risk of heart disease, according to a study published in the November 2001 issue of the *Archives of Internal Medicine*. The study was based on interviews with and medical examinations of more than 9,600 Americans who did not have heart disease when the study began. Over an average of 19 years, about 1,800 cases of coronary heart disease were diagnosed.

People who ate legumes four times a week or more had a 22 percent lower risk of coronary heart disease over 19 years than those who consumed legumes once a week. The most enthusiastic of the legume eaters also had lower blood-pressure and total-cholesterol levels and were less likely to be diagnosed with high blood pressure or diabetes.

Legumes are rich in soluble fiber, low in salt, and high in potassium, calcium, and magnesium (a combination associated with a reduced risk of heart disease). The mineral folate, also found in abundance in legumes, is thought to reduce blood levels of homocysteine.

"Increasing legume consumption may be an important part of dietary interventions to reduce the risk of coronary heart disease," Dr. Lydia A. Bazzano from Tulane University in New Orleans, Louisiana, writes in the research team's summary of the study.

There are, of course, many other foods that contain *insoluble fiber*. According to the AHA, insoluble fiber, which includes grains, doesn't seem to lower blood cholesterol but does appear to protect against heart disease. Whole-wheat breads, wheat cereals, wheat bran, cabbage, beets, carrots, Brussel sprouts, turnips, cauliflower, and apple skin are good examples of foods that provide insoluble fiber.

In general, it's better to get as much fiber as possible from fruits, vegetables, whole-grain foods, beans, and legumes instead of fiber supplements. Foods high in fiber contain other protective substances. There are many types of fiber, and the composition of fiber is poorly understood—which means you might not get everything you need from supplements.

Learn to Read Food Labels

As I've mentioned several times already, the food labels placed on most packaged and canned foods include nutrition facts and the ingredient list. If you're going to be vigilant about lowering your intake of fat, cholesterol and salt, you'll have to learn to understand the language of these labels.

Look at the label and find a section called "Nutrition Facts."

Under the column titled "% Daily Value," you'll be able to see whether a food is high or low in nutrients. If you want to limit a particular nutrient, such as fat, saturated fat, cholesterol, or sodium, choose foods with a lower percentage of that nutrient. If you want to consume more of a nutrient, such as calcium or fiber, try to choose foods with higher percentages of it.

The ingredients listed are in descending order of weight. Note that certain foods contain less nutrient content than the packaging may lead you to believe. For example, many commercial

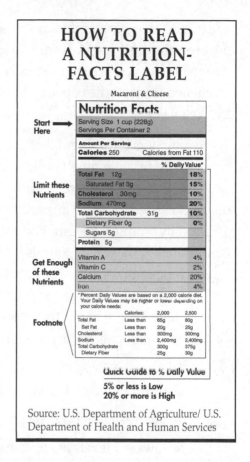

HOW TO READ A NUTRITION-FACTS LABEL

Macaroni & Cheese

Nutrition Facts

Start Here → Serving Size 1 cup (228g)
Servings Per Container 2

Amount Per Serving

Calories 250   Calories from Fat 110

% Daily Value*

Limit these Nutrients		
Total Fat 12g		18%
Saturated Fat 3g		15%
Cholesterol 30mg		10%
Sodium 470mg		20%
Total Carbohydrate 31g		10%
Dietary Fiber 0g		0%
Sugars 5g		
Protein 5g		

Get Enough of these Nutrients	
Vitamin A	4%
Vitamin C	2%
Calcium	20%
Iron	4%

* Percent Daily Values are based on a 2,000 calorie diet. Your Daily Values may be higher or lower depending on your calorie needs:

Footnote
	Calories:	2,000	2,500
Total Fat	Less than	65g	80g
Sat Fat	Less than	20g	25g
Cholesterol	Less than	300mg	300mg
Sodium	Less than	2,400mg	2,400mg
Total Carbohydrate		300g	375g
Dietary Fiber		25g	30g

Quick Guide to % Daily Value

5% or less is Low
20% or more is High

Source: U.S. Department of Agriculture/ U.S. Department of Health and Human Services

oat-bran and wheat-bran products (muffins, chips, and waffles, for example) actually contain very little bran. They may also be high in sodium, total fat, and saturated fat. Reading the labels on all packaged foods keeps your intake of these and other foods in check.

Garlic and the Heart

In one form or another, garlic has been used for centuries for a number of ailments. Some recent studies imply that it can reduce plaque build-up in the arteries. Other studies insist just as adamantly that garlic offers no benefits to the heart and that the positive findings came from clinical studies that were poorly designed. (As you'll see in the next chapter, most of these doubts originated from studies done on garlic supplements, as opposed to fresh cloves.)

Researchers have found that garlic has qualities similar to those of antioxidant vitamins. Garlic contains vitamin A, vitamin C, and selenium, which are antioxidant enzymes that help fight diseases caused, at least in part, by *free radicals*. Free radicals are actually byproducts of our bodies' normal metabolic functions. Unfortunately, these compounds interfere with the ability of certain cells to function normally. They attack and weaken cells and tissues and contribute to disease, and antioxidants help to stop them. (I've included more about the antioxidant vitamins in Chapter 5.) Garlic's antioxidant quality could lead to a number of health benefits.

- improved circulation
- decreased blood pressure
- lowered levels of cholesterol and triglycerides
- improved flexibility of the aorta, which pumps blood to the body from the heart
- reduced platelet stickiness (and thereby a reduced risk of developing blood clots)

The health benefits that fresh garlic appears to offer relate to a sulfur-containing substance called *allicin*. This is activated after the garlic clove is crushed and allowed to sit for about 10 minutes. If you don't mind the odor, you can eat a couple of cloves of garlic a day to get the health benefits. But it's more common to use fresh or *lightly* cooked garlic in meals. But don't overcook it! Overcooking will destroy the beneficial allicin.

For the most part, those who like garlic find it easy to eat some every day. It's safe to eat as much as you want as long as it doesn't give you a stomachache, which is one of its only real drawbacks. As described in the next chapter, you can also take garlic supplements; the benefits, however, may not be as great.

The "Miracle" of Soy

The humble soybean appears to have taken the health-conscious world by storm. Along with oats, it is one of the heart's super stars. Not only does soy contain no fat, but it's also high in protein and is a good source of fiber, B vitamins, calcium, and omega-3 essential fatty acids.

The soybean contains several other disease fighters, including *isoflavones*, *saponins*, and *phytosterols*. Extensive research has been performed on these elements, and here's what makes them such special protectors of our heart:

- *Isoflavones* have antioxidant properties. In other words, they block the action of disease-causing free radicals. In plain English, for example, they can reduce blood clots. Many researchers consider isoflavones to be the key to soy's power.

- *Saponins* are compounds found in a wide variety of vegetables and legumes in addition to soy. They bind to cholesterol (in the gastrointestinal tract) to limit its absorption into the intestines. The cholesterol then passes into the colon to be excreted. This forces the liver to produce more bile acid, which removes cholesterol from the bloodstream and thereby leaves less to build up in the arteries.

■ *Phytosterols* (or sterols) lower cholesterol levels. *Phytostanols* (or stanols) are the synthetic version, which can be found in special cholesterol-lowering margarines and salad dressings now available.

One analysis showed that 89 percent out of a pool of 38 clinical trials reported that a diet high in soy led to cholesterol reductions. Those trials showed that regular soy in your diet helps shave an average of 23 points off total cholesterol levels. Participants in one study took an average of 47 grams of soy daily and had a drop of 9 percent in total cholesterol, a drop of 13 percent in LDL, and a drop of 10 percent in triglycerides.

Because of such generally stellar research results, the FDA has authorized foods containing soy to carry a "heart-healthy" label (just as oatmeal does). The FDA suggests a daily intake of at least 25 grams of soy protein—an amount typically found in about 2 1/2 cups of soy milk or 1/2 pound of tofu—to reduce cholesterol. It also recommends that people with high cholesterol eat more soy every day as part of an overall cholesterol-reducing treatment plan that includes a low-fat diet and, when required, medications.

A concern about soy did surface several years ago when the American College of Nutrition published a study linking large amounts of tofu (two or more servings a week) to cognitive decline later in life. The article summarized a longitudinal study that began in 1965 in which heart disease, stroke, and cancer were examined in a group of Japanese-American men in Hawaii. However, no other studies have found a link between tofu intake and cognitive decline. The current general consensus is that there is no link between them.

In addition to stocking the traditional blocks of white tofu, grocery stores usually carry soy burgers, soy yogurt, soy milk, soy cheese, and many other similar products. Vegetarians have long used tofu as a protein substitute, and those trying to reduce their intake of saturated fats can do the same.

One of the advantages of tofu is its chameleonlike quality; it takes on the taste of the other spices in a dish. It can be stir-fried, steamed with vegetables, or added to soup; in each case, it will take on the flavors that those dishes contain while adding texture and a good dose of protein. Try adding some lemon-pepper tofu to your steamed veggies, cooking some tofu with sun dried tomatoes and basil, or just tossing some of it into your salads. Substitute a slice of soy cheese for your regular slice of cheese on broccoli or toast. Roasted soy nuts, which resemble peanuts, are a delicious crunchy snack.

If you suffer from hyperthyroidism consult your doctor before adding more soy to your diet.

Drink Your OJ

Orange juice has just made a surprising leap into the forefront as a high blood pressure fighter. Researchers in the department of cardiovascular medicine at the Cleveland Clinic recently announced the results of their JUICE ("Juice utilization improves cardiovascular endpoints") study at the annual scientific session of the American College of Cardiology.

Study participants were given four different beverages—three of which were different brands of 100% orange juice—for two weeks each. The subjects, who had a partial blockage in the arteries leading to their hearts, were taken off of all medications immediately before each of their clinic visits. They drank two 16-ounce glasses of the test beverage daily. At the end of each of the two-week periods, measurements were taken of blood pressure and brachial-artery reactivity (an indicator of the flexibility of vessels).

The results of the study clearly demonstrated that drinking two glasses of orange juice a day for six weeks leads to a significant reduction in blood pressure. Previous studies had shown that a number of nutrients that naturally occur in orange juice, such as potassium, vitamin C, and other antioxidants, do have a beneficial effect on blood pressure. However, this is the first time that research has shown that an everyday food can lower blood pressure.

But What About Dessert?

As indicated by the food-guide pyramid mentioned earlier, sweets are among the foods people are advised to use sparingly— and there are several reasons for this. Eating sugar has been reported to reduce protective HDL cholesterol and increase various heart-disease risk factors, such as being overweight.

Among the major sources of sugar consumption in the American diet are soft drinks. In fact, the average American consumes about 20 teaspoons of added sugar per day instead of the 10 teaspoons recommended by the dietary guidelines. (The "added" refers to the amount beyond what naturally occurs in foods, such as fruits.)

One recently published study found that individuals who adopt a low-fat diet tend to replace fats with simple sugars in non-fat baked goods and processed foods. Simple sugars can reduce HDL levels, and low HDL levels are known to be a major heart-disease risk factor for women.

"The current American food supply offers an abundance of low-fat and fat-free foods that depend on simple carbohydrates or added sugars to improve their flavor," Linda B. Bunyard and colleagues from the University of Maryland at Baltimore write in the *Journal of the American Dietetic Association*. "Whether the recent trend toward fat-modified foods provides an overall benefit to this population is questionable."

In this study, 55 overweight postmenopausal white women followed the AHA's step-I diet—which includes less than 30 percent of the total calories from fat. After 10 weeks, the women lost an average of 2 percent of their body weight, reduced their total cholesterol by 8 percent, and cut their LDL cholesterol by 6 percent. HDL, or "good," cholesterol declined 16 percent, however.

During the same period, the women's average intakes of total fat, saturated fat, and cholesterol fell, while the percent of calories from carbohydrates (complex carbohydrates like whole grains and simple sugars) rose. According to the analysis, a higher average intake of simple sugars was the only dietary change associated with lower HDL.

The moral of the story is that people who succeed on a low-fat diet by substituting simple sugars may be at risk of lowering their HDL cholesterol. The researchers stressed that their findings do not suggest that individuals avoid fruits and vegetables, which contain natural sugar.

Marion Nestle, chairperson of the department of nutrition and food studies at New York University, chimes in on that same note: "Because sugary foods often replace more healthful foods, diets high in sugar are almost certainly contributing to osteoporosis, cancer, and heart disease."

This doesn't mean that you can never have another dessert, but just don't go overboard. If you must have something sweet, and many of us must, choose carefully and eat less. Remember: Moderation is key.

On a positive note, recent studies have found that *moderate* amounts of pure chocolate contain flavonoids. (I discuss this in more depth in the next chapter.) Most of the fat in chocolate is stearic acid, however, which is a fatty acid that does raise cholesterol even when eaten in *moderate* amounts. Furthermore, chocolate contains a lot of calories—so be careful!

Go Easy on the Alcohol

The general rule from health experts on drinking alcohol is to do so in moderation. That means no more than one drink per day for women and no more than two drinks for men. Although too much alcohol may raise cholesterol and triglyceride levels in the blood, many researchers cite its positive side.

- It raises HDL cholesterol levels.

- It lowers blood pressure.

- It provides antioxidant effects, which help prevent artery damage.

- It inhibits the formation of blood clots in the coronary arteries.

According to the American Heart Association, people who drink moderately have heart disease less often than do non-drinkers. When people drink too much alcohol or drink it too often, however, their blood pressure sometimes increases.

Red wine has been the subject of major research, because it appears to protect the heart. Researchers believe that heart disease and high cholesterol are caused, at least in part, by free-radical damage to blood vessels. Because red wine contains certain antioxidants that protect the heart from this activity, it is of particular interest. Research has been done on several of its heart-healthy compounds, including quercetin and polyphenols.

Findings of a study published in the journal *Nature*, for example, support the theory that *polyphenols*, which are found in red-grape skins, decrease the production of a protein that causes blood vessels to constrict and reduce oxygen flow to the heart. According to researcher Dr. Roger Corder and colleagues from Queen Mary University of London, England, the protein (endothelin-1) plays a role in the development of heart disease.

Although they are present in red-grape juice also, the polyphenols are not as potent and do not have quite as dramatic an effect on lowering the protein as they do in red wine. Researchers believe that something in the winemaking process raises the positive polyphenols. This doesn't seem to occur in white wine, however, possibly because the grape skins do not contain the same compounds.

"Consumption of up to two glasses of red wine per day with food might be considered part of a diet to reduce heart disease," Corder said. Naturally, neither Corder nor any other researcher advocates taking up drinking alcohol to get its preventive benefits. In all cases, any benefits of wine and other alcohol should be balanced with their potential risks. The key is to drink them, if you do so at all, in moderation.

Coffee or Tea?

Some evidence suggests that high amounts of caffeine can cause irregular heart rhythms (arrhythmias), and other research finds that caffeine can increase homocysteine levels. For these reasons, some physicians advise their heart patients, particularly those who have already had a heart attack, to drink little to no coffee. Many, however, consider the evidence on this to be weak, so don't panic if you're among the 50 percent of Americans who need a few cups of coffee every day. In fact, researchers at Johns Hopkins University recently completed a long-term study on the possible link between hypertension and coffee that spanned three entire decades. The report, which was detailed in the March 2002 issue of the *Archives of Internal Medicine,* concluded that drinking an average of two cups of coffee a day probably does not play any significant role in causing high blood pressure. In fact, according to one of the study's authors, there has yet to be a single study finding such a link between coffee and high blood pressure, despite over 60 years of the theory's being kicked around the scientific and medical communities.

Many recent studies have declared both black and green teas (which come from the same plant, by the way) to be potential heart tonics. Once again, tea's antioxidant properties are the reasons why it is thought to be beneficial for the heart.

A study conducted in the Netherlands over a 10-year period showed that men who consumed three cups of black tea per day were less likely to die of ischemic heart disease than those who consumed just half a cup. Similarly, green tea has been reported to have the ability to reduce atherosclerosis and high cholesterol levels.

According to findings from several other studies, green tea "mildly" lowered LDL cholesterol and increased HDL cholesterol. It also increased antioxidant activity in the blood and made platelets in the blood less sticky. The evidence that green tea also protects again atherosclerosis, however, is still considered preliminary.

If you want the full benefits of green tea, you'll have to drink *at least* three cups a day to get them. In Chapter 5, I talk more about why green tea or extracts of green tea can be so special.

Speaking to the Exceptions

The things I've said above about dietary habits will help everyone's overall health, whether there's a cholesterol problem or not.

But I'd like to note for the record that 20 percent of the adult population consists of what researchers call "non-responders." Their cholesterol levels won't budge (drop) no matter how strict their diet and exercise regimens might be. But the many other positive health results that can be obtained through diet and exercise still make them invaluable tools for reaching optimum health.

On the other hand, 20 percent of us will never have to worry about high cholesterol no matter what we eat. (I cite an interesting study at the end of Chapter 6 about a unique nomadic tribe in Africa the members of which fit this description.) But as I said at the start of this chapter, most of us will face the battle of cholesterol at some point in our lives. In addition to the many dietary interventions I have covered here, there are vitamin and herbal supplements that will help. I review these in the next chapter.

CHAPTER 5

Vitamins and Herbs for Your Heart

There's no substitute for a diet that's low in saturated fats and high in fruits, vegetables, and grains. For many people, though, that's not enough to fight heart disease, and they require what one nutritionist calls a little more "insurance." There are several natural forms this insurance could take, including supplements of vitamins, minerals, and herbs. And remember that they *supplement* a good diet; they don't replace one.

Most of these natural products are considered "safe" when you stick to commonly recommended dosages. And, as you'll see, there are many vitamins and herbs that could help your heart, and there's a lot to learn about each one. If you're serious about using therapeutic dosages of vitamins and herbs, working with a professional who's an expert on them is a good idea. This advice is doubly important for those who have already had a heart attack or are at high risk of heart disease. In fact, in such a case, be sure to let your doctor know that you intend to add supplements to your diet.

We are lucky to live in a time when highly trained medical doctors are learning to work within the realm of an "alternative" treatment. I'm talking about physicians and other providers who work in the area of *integrative medicine.* Such individuals can offer you help beyond traditional modern medicine. Alternative therapies, which include supplements, are accepted as a part of this new encompassing field of medicine.

"Natural" Doesn't Mean Risk-free

Although vitamins and minerals will probably produce fewer side effects and consequences than do prescription drugs, there are still a few things to remember about them.

- If you're taking any prescription drugs, especially for your heart, do some research on whether the supplement can cause any side effects. Some vitamins and herbs can enhance or halt the effect of prescription medications, and this is obviously something you want to avoid.

- Don't go overboard when you're taking supplements. It's easy to forget that even these natural products can be harmful when we take too much. I've listed some of the commonly held beliefs about "safe" and recommended dosages below, but it's important that you always read the labels and consult with an expert before diving into larger-than-recommended dosages.

- Be aware that some vitamins don't have official dosage limits because researchers haven't found that they cause harm. This doesn't mean they couldn't, so stay cautious about your intake of them.

- When buying vitamins, you may have a choice of natural or synthetic versions (organic or inorganic). Some experts recommend natural sources because they may be more potent and easier for your body to use.

- Some vitamins and minerals work better when taken together, and I've provided this information whenever it has been available.

Step 1: Take a Multivitamin. According to most health experts, everyone should take a multivitamin every day—and that includes anyone concerned about heart disease. To find out how much you're taking, check for the *recommended daily allowance (RDA)* or *daily value (DV)* on the bottle. The DV is a newer government standard that corresponds closely to the RDA. The point of both is to show consumers the minimum daily requirements.

Levels higher than these, often called extra-strength formulas, may help prevent or delay chronic diseases like those of the heart. People over 50, for example, should look for multivitamins that include vitamins B_6 and B_{12} in the higher ranges. As we age, our bodies have a harder time absorbing these nutrients. Extra calcium (up to 1,200 mg a day) and vitamin D (400 to 600 IUs daily) also might help if you're over 50.

Step 2: Focus on the Heart. A lot of research has been done on whether extra-supplement formulas do prevent, or should be used to treat, heart disease. Although conclusions from clinical studies vary about the benefits of taking individual vitamins, most physicians and other health-care providers believe that in most cases the extra amount won't hurt. Although research continues on what helps the heart and what doesn't, the following seem to be the front-runners for daily, healthy-heart supplements.

- antioxidants: betacarotene (vitamin A), coenzyme Q_{10}, vitamin C, vitamin E, and selenium (a trace element)

- Three of the B vitamins: vitamin B_6, vitamin B_{12}, and folic acid

- calcium (a mineral)

- magnesium (a mineral)

In addition to these widely accepted "stars," there are other important vitamins to consider. I've included several of these below.

Antioxidants

If you're eating five to 10 servings of fruits and vegetables a day and taking a multivitamin, you might be getting the amount of antioxidants your body needs. But, then again, you might not be. It won't hurt, and it might help, to supplement your diet even further with the antioxidants that have shown the most heart-friendly benefits: vitamin A (especially betacarotene), coenzyme Q_{10}, vitamin C, vitamin E, and selenium. Some heart experts also throw a few others into what has been called an "antioxidant cocktail."

As you might expect, antioxidants got their name because they choke off, or neutralize, the oxygen needed by *free radicals*—potentially damaging byproducts from the body's metabolism and from air pollution. Free radicals attack and weaken cells and tissues and contribute to disease, and antioxidants help to stop them.

In the case of the heart, for example, free radicals play a big role in low-density-lipoprotein (LDL) cholesterol levels. Researchers believe that the LDL molecules become dangerous only when they are damaged by free radicals. A Japanese study found that levels of oxidized LDL cholesterol were four times higher in heart-attack victims than in healthy people.

Some antioxidants are found in food, and the body produces some naturally. When taken as supplements, they seem to work best when taken together, according, at least, to the leading antioxidant researchers. For example, Lester Packer, Ph.D., a professor of molecular and cell biology at the University of California, Berkeley, believes there's an "antioxidant network." Packer and his colleagues recommend a balanced mix of these vitamins to ensure that all parts of the body are protected and also because not everyone reacts to each one in the same way.

You can get the benefits of antioxidants by eating foods or taking supplements rich in *flavonoids*, which come in many different categories. The isoflavones found in soy constitute one common type, and there are many others. Like other antioxidants, flavonoids protect LDL cholesterol from damaging free radicals and other occurrences that lead to heart disease.

Alpha-Lipoic Acid. When we hit our 40s and 50s, our bodies' production of this "universal antioxidant" declines; it therefore becomes important that we get it from food and supplements. It's known as "universal" because, unlike other antioxidants, it dissolves in both water and fat. This gives it the ability to stop free-radical cells floating around in tissues made mostly of water, such as the heart, and made mostly of fat, such as the nervous system. Other antioxidants don't have this flexibility.

The best way to get alpha-lipoic acid is through dietary sources, such as spinach, beef, and potatoes, and brewer's yeast. It's also sold as a single supplement and in combination with other antioxidants. For general protection, most experts recommend around 100 mg twice a day.

Coenzyme Q_{10}. This vitaminlike nutrient is found in every cell of the body, but levels decrease as we get older—so supplements become essential. In addition to serving as an antioxidant, coenzyme Q_{10} helps to convert food into energy. It is found in high amounts in a healthy heart. Researchers say that 75 percent of the people with heart disease have low levels of this enzyme.

Research on coenzyme Q_{10} and its positive effects on the heart has been under way for decades. It is now considered to be a good treatment for the early stages of congestive heart failure (within a year or two of diagnosis) when used in high enough dosages. It improves the function of the healthy part of the heart (i.e., the part that's left after CHF damage). Preliminary evidence also shows that its antioxidant properties slow the damaging effects of LDL cholesterol.

Coenzyme Q_{10} is one of the top 10 medications sold in Japan, and it's also widely used in parts of Europe. American health-care providers are finally acknowledging its benefits and are jumping on the coenzyme-Q_{10} bandwagon, although more cautiously. Some physicians recommend using it along with conventional treatments, especially with cholesterol-lowering drugs.

In spite of coenzyme Q_{10}'s effectiveness, many people (including doctors) haven't even heard of it. If it is so effective in the treatment of heart failure, why is it not more generally used in this country? In response to this question, the International Coenzyme Q_{10} Association posted this on its Website.

"The answer to this question is found in the fields of politics and marketing and not in the fields of science and medicine. The controversy surrounding coenzyme Q_{10} likewise is political and economic, as the previous 30 years of research...have been remarkably consistent and free of major controversy."

Most of us are deficient in coenzyme Q_{10}, and supplements can provide what's missing. Clinical trials have shown positive responses to as little as 30 mg to 50 mg per day and to as much as 400 mg. Because this is a fat-soluble vitamin, it is best when chewed with a fat-containing food.

Vitamin A. This fat-soluble vitamin is actually derived from various *carotenoids* (the pigments that color some vegetables and fruits). Although there are 600 or so of these natural plant compounds, the body uses only about six of them in any significant way. The one we're most familiar with is betacarotene, which shows up in all of the foods where the other six prominent carotenoids are found.

FOODS RICH IN VITAMIN A	
5 oz. sweet potato	15,000 IU
2 to 3 apricots	15,000 IU
1 cup peas and carrots	15,000 IU
1 cup baked butternut squash	13,000 IU
1 raw carrot	5,000 IU
1/2 mango	4,800 IU
1/4 cantaloupe	3,500 IU
1 stalk broccoli	3,500 IU
1 raw tomato	1,800 IU
1/3 papaya	1,750 IU
IU = international unit	

Researchers have found that people who have high levels of vitamin A in their blood have a decreased risk of heart disease and also have better outcomes after strokes. One research team, for example, evaluated 1,300 people and found that those who ate the most carotenoid-rich foods were 75 percent less likely to have a heart attack.

The best way get the required amount of vitamin A is through fruits and vegetables—at least five servings a day. You'll find carotenes in foods like carrots, sweet potatoes, squash, spinach, broccoli, pumpkins, kale, and sweet red peppers.

Vitamin A is also found in a plant that most of us wouldn't think to include in our salads or on sandwiches—dandelion leaves! These have the highest vitamin A content of all greens. As an added bonus, they're a good source of potassium. They also act as a light diuretic, which may help people with mild cases of high blood pressure or CHF by relieving some of the fluid build-up. If you choose to pick your own dandelion leaves, just be sure that they come from a location you are sure has not been exposed to pesticides.

Vitamin A is one of those supplements that could be toxic at high levels. If you do decide to use supplements, stick to conservative doses. The DV for vitamin A is 5,000 international units (IU's).

Vitamin C. In its role as an antioxidant, vitamin C protects the heart against damage from LDL cholesterol. For the heart, however, it seems to work best when taken with other antioxidants in a sort of "antioxidant cocktail." Many researchers, including the AHA, believe the best sources of vitamin C are fruits and vegetables rather than supplements.

According to one researcher, people who eat a lot of vegetables have a significantly reduced risk of stroke. He evaluated individuals who took vitamin C and those who consume a lot of vegetables. While the stroke risk fell in both groups, "the risk of all types of stroke was 58 percent lower among those who consumed vegetables six to seven days per week." These findings give us a message that we've heard all our lives: Eat your vegetables.

Dosages of 1,000 mg are thought to be safe, but cardioprotective benefits of vitamin C can be had with as little as 100 mg per day.

Vitamin E. Studies on vitamin E seem to be in the current spotlight, and the reviews are mixed on how much it decreases one's risk of heart disease. According to Dr. Lester Packer, as many as 30 percent of people taking it don't respond to its heart-protecting properties (of course that leaves another 70 percent who do).

In the early 1990s, a study conducted at Harvard University showed that men who took vitamin E had a 35 percent lower risk of heart disease. Another study "proved" that even modest amounts of vitamin E could protect against ischemic stroke.

Then there was the study of 25,000 people who did not show significant benefits from taking vitamin E as a dietary supplement for the prevention of coronary heart disease. A smaller study combined antioxidants with two cholesterol-lowering drugs, and researchers said the vitamins made "no significant dent" in patients' heart risks.

Yet another study proved that a low dose of aspirin had more cardioprotective ability than vitamin E.

In spite of the mixed reviews of vitamin E, numerous researchers do believe it can increase high-density lipoprotein (HDL)—the good cholesterol—and decrease LDL cholesterol. The

AHA, however, doesn't share this view, saying that the positive findings occurred only with very high dosages.

Another complication to the vitamin E issue is that there are two categories or types of vitamin E. The one most of us take is *tocopherol*; the other is tocotrienol. The first category has been more widely studied, but tocotrienols are now being touted as the more powerful of the two. The evidence that these will lower blood cholesterol is no less conflicting than that for the first category, although some studies show significant drops in cholesterol levels. For example, one study showed 15 percent less total cholesterol after 28 days and 8 percent less LDL cholesterol.

Since tocopherols and tocotrienols seem to offer slightly different benefits, the experts advise simply taking both. Supplements are a good alternative, since to ingest 200 units of vitamin E, you would have to consume 10 cups of almonds, which are its richest food source. A daily safe dose is 1,200 units, although much less (400 to 800 units of tocopherols and 100 mg of tocotrienols) also may be helpful in reducing heart-disease risk.

Selenium. Selenium is one of the essential trace minerals in the human body. Lack of this mineral in the blood has been connected to low HDL levels and an increased risk of heart attacks. Sufficient selenium levels are essential for the immune system to function properly. Selenium definitely helps the antioxidants do their job, but this is another case of not wanting to get too much of a good thing. In large dosages, selenium might harm the liver and nervous system. Stick to somewhere between 70 micrograms and 100 micrograms (mcg) in a supplement, but don't take more than 200 mcg daily.

Selenium, which is found naturally in rocks and soil, is passed into the foods we eat. The mineral is severely depleted, however, in many areas and the amounts present in food grown in selenium-deficient soil or animals that eat plant food in these depleted areas can be significantly low. You can add more selenium naturally to your diet by eating foods typically higher in the mineral, such as meats, whole-grain breads, walnuts and Brazil nuts.

Food Sources of Antioxidants

- *Coenzyme Q_{10}:* It's present in a lot of foods, including beef, soy oil, sardines, mackerel, and nuts. (It's also found in organ meats, such as heart, liver, and kidney, but because these are extra high in dietary cholesterol and saturated fat, you should try to limit these foods.)

- *Vitamin A:* Dairy products; orange vegetables, such as sweet potatoes, carrots, mangos, and cantaloupe; dark-green vegetables like spinach, kale, broccoli, collard greens, and dandelion leaves; yellow fruits, such as peaches, apricots and papaya; and fish-liver oils are all good sources.

- *Vitamin C:* Citrus fruits like oranges, grapefruits, and lemons, as well as many other fruits and vegetables, particularly strawberries, potatoes, tomatoes, red chili peppers, sweet peppers, cauliflower, and cabbage, are all good sources.

- *Vitamin E:* Sources include almonds, avocados, brown rice, walnuts, wheat-germ oil, whole grains, green leafy vegetables, rice bran, corn, soybeans, and various vegetable oils, including safflower oil and sunflower oil.

■ *Selenium:* Eggs, chicken, garlic, onions, seafood, whole grains, wheat germ, nuts, oats, brown rice, turnips, barley, orange juice, broccoli, cabbage, and celery are all good sources. (Note that the selenium content in plants varies depending on the kind of soil they're grown in.)

Arginine

Arginine is a naturally occurring amino acid that appears to help restore normal blood pressure for some people who have mild hypertension. Some researchers even say it lowers cholesterol, opens clogged arteries, and reduces angina. You might wonder how one simple mineral—one that most of us haven't even heard of—could do all of this.

Its positive affects on the heart appear to be connected with the fact that it boosts nitric oxide in the cells that line the blood vessels. Nitric oxide expands or relaxes the vessels so blood can flow freely, and this helps relieve angina and even lowers blood pressure. Three American scientists won the 1998 Nobel Prize for Medicine for their discovery of nitric oxide's crucial role in the heart.

A book by physicians Robert Fried and Woodson C. Merrell called *The Arginine Solution* explains the arginine/nitric-oxcide connection. When people age and develop disorders like elevated cholesterol, their bodies lose some of the ability to convert arginine to nitric oxide. Fried and Merrell contend that taking supplements of arginine can improve this ability and thus decrease cardiovascular disorders. Many other researchers have found that supplements of arginine have positive effects on the cardiovascular system, improving many of the conditions we have discussed.

Arginine is not a miracle supplement, though, and it should be approached cautiously, especially if you're already taking medications. Watchdogs say that no one really knows what high amounts of this isolated amino acid will do to the body, especially over the long term. They also say that if arginine supplements are as good as they claim to be, they're drugs rather than supplements. This may be a distinction to discuss with your physician or knowledgeable health-care provider before you decide to take arginine.

Supplements are sold as L-arginine, and a total of 3 grams a day (1 gram three times a day) is a common recommendation. Don't expect results for at least one or two months. Also, avoid taking arginine if you're taking any other medications, such as nitroglycerin, that widen blood vessels.

B vitamins

It appears that the B vitamins are involved in hundreds of reactions in our bodies, including those that involve the cardiovascular system. One of their most important functions is to help control homocysteine levels in the blood. Researchers keep trying to determine exactly which B vitamin is the best for the heart, but the evidence is conflicting. For example, there's research indicating that vitamin B_6 is the key helper nutrient for normalizing homocysteine levels, but there's also research showing that folic acid is the key. A recent study done in Ireland suggests that fortifying certain foods with vitamin B_{12} in addition to folic acid could help reduce rates of heart disease. Your best bet for getting what you need is to take a good B-complex vitamin.

Like the antioxidants, the B vitamins do seem to work best as a team; this is particularly true in the area of lowering high homocysteine levels in the blood. Researchers have found, however, that vitamin B_6, vitamin B_{12} and folic acid (or folate)—when taken together—are the leaders. When adequate amounts of these three are found in the blood, homocysteine levels fall. When these vitamins are lacking, homocysteine often builds up to become a risk factor for heart disease.

The Nurses' Health Study was one of the largest long-term clinical studies ever performed. A total of 80,000 women with no history of heart disease were studied for connections linking vitamin B_6, folic acid, and heart disease. The researchers concluded that B_6 supplements significantly reduced a woman's risk and that folic acid was also effective.

Another study found that people with the highest B_6 levels in the blood were 28 percent less likely to develop heart disease. In this case, the protective benefit turned out to be not a lower homocysteine level but a higher level of B_6. The fact that homocysteine was lowered was incidental, said the researchers.

Since it's difficult to get enough B vitamins from your diet, a wide range of health experts advise supplement use. Start with a multivitamin that includes B and then check out the many specialized B-complex formulas available. For those of you who plan to go for extra doses of the vitamin-B leaders, here's a breakdown of safe daily dosages:

- Vitamin B_6 (pyridoxine): 50 mg to 200 mg (never exceed 500 mg.)

- Vitamin B_{12}: 50 micrograms (mcg) to 3,000 mcg

- Folic acid: 400 mcg to 1,000 mcg

Although niacin (the nicotinic-acid version) is not always recommended as part of the heart-healthy B-vitamin family, be sure the complex you take includes some. Like the others, it's often recommended to lower cholesterol. Note that nicotinamide (also called niacinamide), a similar type of this B vitamin, doesn't seem to have the same effect.

Food Sources of the B Vitamins

- *Vitamin B$_6$:* beef, beer, chicken, milk, and tuna

- *Vitamin B$_{12}$:* fortified cereals, fish, pork, and eggs

- *Folic acid:* green leafy vegetables, beans, peas, chicken giblets, orange juice, liver, and peanuts. Also, many breads, cereals, and flours, as well as pasta and rice, have been fortified with folic acid.

Brewer's yeast. I'll bet you've all heard of brewer's yeast, which is best known as a rich source of B-complex vitamins. It also contains a readily absorbable (or biologically active) form of **chromium,** an essential trace mineral. In fact, true brewer's yeast is considered the best source of chromium.

Studies have shown that brewer's-yeast supplements reduce LDL cholesterol and increase HDL cholesterol. Researchers have found that people with high levels of chromium in their blood have a lower risk of heart disease.

Brewer's yeast can be taken as a powder or in tablet or capsule form. High-quality brewer's yeast contains as much as 60 mcg of chromium per tablespoon. When doctors recommend it, they suggest 1 to 2 tablespoons per day. Others double that dosage so that their patients can get at least 200 mcg of chromium a day.

When buying, be sure to look for labels that say "from the brewing process" or "brewer's yeast." Other types of yeast aren't what you want. True brewer's yeast has a very bitter taste, so if you get the powder and don't experience that taste, check it again, as you may have the wrong kind.

Betaine

Like the B vitamins, this is another homocysteine fighter—though one that we hear little about. This organic compound is a by-product of sugar-beet processing. It works closely with folic acid, vitamin B_{12}, and choline (an essential nutrient found in many multivitamins and B-complex vitamins that helps move fats in and out of cells). Betaine (trimethylglycine) is used therapeutically to prevent the build-up of homocysteine; this, in turn, helps fight heart disease, stroke, and peripheral vascular disease. Doctors sometimes recommend betaine for people who have taken folic acid, vitamin B_6, and vitamin B_{12} to lower elevated homocysteine levels but who haven't had any luck with them.

If you're not getting enough B vitamins from fruits and vegetables, consider supplements that either include either the betaine-citrate or the betaine-aspartate variety. The appropriate dosage varies according to the reason it's being used. For example a dosage of 500 mg to 1,000 mg a day is often recommended for general cardiovascular health, although in special cases, up to 6 grams per day may be warranted. Supplements are available in powder, capsule, and tablet form. Be sure you get the betaine-citrate kind or the betaine aspartate variety and not the betaine-hydrochloride version. Dietary sources of this vitamin include fish, broccoli, spinach, beets, and legumes.

Calcium

Calcium is the most abundant mineral in the body. Most of the calcium in our bodies is stored in our bones, but it is the small amount that is present in the blood that makes a big difference to the heart. Calcium deficiency, which is present in most Americans, appears to mildly increase blood-pressure levels, and supplemental calcium appears to reduce total and LDL cholesterol by about 4 percent and raise HDL cholesterol by a similar amount.

Researchers have found that adequate calcium keeps the walls of the blood vessels flexible and supports the hormones that help them contract. These actions help keep blood pressure within the normal range, even when salt is consumed.

Calcium also appears to lower cholesterol by slowing the amount of saturated fats being absorbed from the stomach into the bloodstream. With the help of calcium, some of these saturated fats can be harmlessly released from the body as waste products and thus lower cholesterol over time.

It's hard to get enough calcium from food, so supplements are probably needed. Recommended dosages generally hover around 1,000 mg for adults, though up to 2,500 mg per day can be considered safe. Studies have found that our bodies can't absorb more than 500 mg of calcium at one time, so it's best to take two or more doses daily. Make sure you are getting sufficient amounts of magnesium in your diet as well. In order to properly absorb and utilize calcium, magnesium must be present in the body.

Food sources of calcium include dairy products (e.g., skim milk and cheese), orange juice or soy milk fortified with calcium, salmon, fish canned with its bones (such as sardines), calcium-processed tofu, dark-green vegetables, and seeds.

Fish Oil

If you're not a "fish person," you might be able to get the benefits that fish brings by taking supplements. Fish oil contains two types of omega-3 fatty acids: eicosapentanoic acid (EPA) and docosahexanoic acid (DHA). When you look for supplements, check to be sure that the one you choose contains about 18 percent EPA and 12 percent DHA or a total of 30 percent omega-3.

Like fish, supplements may help lower triglycerides and blood pressure.

Before you take fish-oil supplements, you may want to check with your doctor. The general belief is that one needs at least 3 grams of EPA plus DHA, and that's a lot of fish oil! Elevated blood-sugar and cholesterol levels have occurred in some people taking these supplements. Obviously, this defeats the purpose; you may decide to just learn to like fish.

Garlic

As I already explained in Chapter 4, cloves of the garlic plant are frequently used, and enjoyed, in cooking. Garlic has been around for thousands of years, both as a food and as a traditional Chinese medicine. Partly because of its longevity, scientists have taken garlic's benefits seriously. Hundreds of studies have been conducted over the last 15 years or so.

From all reports, the top advantage of garlic is its promise to reduce atherosclerosis. One group of researchers conducted a clinical trial on a group of people who ranged in age from 50 to 80 and already had hardening of the arteries. Every day for four years, part of the group took 900 mg of a *standardized* garlic-powder supplement and part took a placebo. At the end of the study, researchers found that those who took garlic had an average reduction in plaque volume of 4.5 percent. The plaque volume of the placebo group increased by about 15 percent.

As mentioned in Chapter 4, it is the *allicin* that makes garlic work for the heart. Although there have been numerous positive findings about garlic's benefit, there have also been studies with mixed results. One reason given for this lack of consistency is that the amount of *allicin* found in garlic supplements varies, and so has the amount given to clinical-trial participants. This being the case, it's hard to make comparisons about what works and what doesn't. As one analyst noted, some of the studies used aged garlic extracts or garlic oil that didn't even contain allicin, and, perhaps predictably, the cholesterol levels in humans were not lowered.

It's important to read the label of any product you buy to be sure you're getting a standardized dose of allicin. A typical dosage recommendation is 600 mg to 900 mg daily in two or three divided doses; this will give you up to 2,000 mcg of potential allicin. Some experts feel that capsules providing 1,000 mg to 3,000 mg are appropriate to take on a daily basis. For those taking garlic oil, a typical dosage is about 0.12 mL three times a day.

If you decide to use garlic supplements, be sure you get the enteric-coated variety so that the garlic doesn't break down within the stomach before it can pass into the small intestine to be absorbed. Also, be aware that garlic supplements are not recommended for those with bleeding or blood-clotting disorders or those who take blood-thinning medications (anticoagulants). Garlic also may cause negative reactions when it's mixed with aspirin, antacids, Ginkgo biloba, laxatives, or supplements with high doses of vitamin C. Those who are scheduled for surgery also may be advised to stop taking garlic supplements.

L-carnitine

The vitaminlike L-carnitine's primary role in the body is to transport fatty acids into the mitochondria situated in the cytoplasm of cells. These mitochondria are sites where energy is manufactured. Since the heart needs a lot of energy, it's easy to see why we wouldn't want to be deficient in this vitamin. Most North Americans are not deficient in L-carnitine; however, researchers have found that many people with heart disease *are*, in fact, deficient. One theory is that they are unable to use the type that is found naturally in some foods and thus may need to be taking supplements of it.

Research has revealed that L-carnitine (LC) is needed for several different aspects of heart health. Doctors, in fact, are now regularly using it for a variety of heart-related conditions. It has been used to relieve angina, treat arrhythmias, and lower LDL-cholesterol and trigylceride levels while increasing HDL cholesterol. In addition, the nutrient, which is depleted in the cardiac muscle during a heart attack, has even been used to reduce the damage *after* a heart attack has occurred.

It sounds like an overall winner for the heart, doesn't it? The nutrient is primarily found in red meats and other animal-based foods, such as fish, poultry, and milk products. Luckily for those who are trying to reduce their intake of animal products, it's also found in soybeans, wheat, and avocados.

The U.S. Food and Drug Administration has approved some LC products for medical use; if you're suffering from a serious deficiency, your physician may prescribe these. However, the lighter versions of LC are sold as supplements. To treat heart disease, a total amount of between 600 mg and 2,500 mg a day is often recommended. Be sure to divide this into two or three doses throughout the day to aid in absorption.

Magnesium

Our bodies use magnesium, a mineral, for a number of purposes. Our hearts need it to function properly, and people with congestive heart failure have an even greater need for it. Because of its ability to block calcium from entering muscle and heart cells, it's sometimes referred to as "nature's calcium channel blocker" (after prescription drugs of the same name). Used over time, magnesium may lower high blood pressure.

Various researchers believe that a person's magnesium levels help determine whether he or she will survive a heart attack. The heart seems to age more quickly when one has low levels of magnesium in the blood. This may cause a number of problems, including chest pain (angina) from clogged arteries, heart attacks, high blood pressure, arrhythmias, and strokes. However, it is important to note that **one** clinical trial found that people with a history of heart disease who were assigned to magnesium supplements experienced more heart attacks, so if you're concerned, get the magnesium you need through the foods you eat.

Magnesium also blocks the release of a hormone that constricts the blood vessels. By doing this, it appears to inhibit blood clots and to help keep blood vessels open, a process that, of course, maximizes blood flow. Working together with calcium and potassium, it regulates blood pressure.

Several studies suggest that magnesium supplements might reduce blood pressure in people with hypertension. It's generally considered safe to take dosages of 1,500 mg but not over 2,500 mg. However, a dosage of about 450 or so mg per day is adequate for heart protection.

Food sources of magnesium include dark-green vegetables, fish, "hard" water, sunflower seeds, nuts, whole grains, kelp, wheat bran and germ, nuts, almonds, cashews, avocados, sweet corn, cheddar cheese, shrimp, and dried fruit.

Soy Supplements

You'll remember from the previous chapter that the humble soybean seems to be able to lower high cholesterol. If soy products (like tofu and miso) aren't your cup of tea, you do have the option of a supplement. Soy powders and soy concentrates are probably better choices than tablets and capsules if you want to listen to the notes of concern raised by some experts.

There is a concern that supplements of *isolated* soy components (such as isoflavones)—the kind that come in tablets and capsules—may not be safe. The bottom line, these folks say, is that you don't know what you're getting in the supplements and you don't know how much of it you're getting. Researchers don't conclusively know, for example, that isoflavones are *the* reason that soy products lower cholesterol. Most of the research has been done on people who have eaten foods rich in soy for many years, and soy foods contain many components besides isoflavones.

However, on the flip side of this coin, researchers have found that supplements containing high amounts of isoflavones (more than 27 mg in a daily dose) do lower total cholesterol and LDL cholesterol. Other studies show that preparations lower in isoflavones don't seem to lower cholesterol levels.

In addition to containing isoflavones, soy contains components called *phytosterols*. You might find that soy supplements indicate that they contain beta-sitosterol, which blocks—and thus reduces—the body's absorption of cholesterol. It's found in almost all plants and can be obtained from rice bran, wheat germ, corn oil, and soybeans.

Research has shown that soy preparations containing high amounts of isoflavones effectively lower total-cholesterol and LDL-cholesterol levels. On the other hand, low-isoflavone preparations (those containing less than 25 mg in a daily dose) did not do so in clinical trials. Studies on phytosterol, a component of soy that blocks cholesterol absorption, also have shown good results.

One study evaluated 0.8, 1.6, and 3.2 grams of plant sterols per day. Researchers discovered that the higher the intake, the more the patient's cholesterol dropped.

The ideal intake for lowering cholesterol is not known, but, as stated in Chapter 4, a total of 25 grams of soy protein per day is generally recommended, although even a total of just 20 grams a day has been shown to help lower cholesterol levels. Many say that you're better off if you get your soy from food products. But whether you just eat soy foods or take supplements, don't go overboard consuming it. As with most things, moderation is the key.

Heart-healthy Herbs

Herbal supplements have been used for thousands of years for medicinal purposes. These supplements are made from various parts of plants: leaves, stems, roots, bark, buds, and flowers. Some are used in their natural form, while others are refined into tablets, capsules, powders, and tinctures. Researchers have found that several herbs, sometimes taken alone and sometimes in combination, offer benefits for the function of the heart.

People who "prescribe" herbs include naturopaths, acupuncturists, holistic doctors, and a growing number of mainstream physicians. Herbal prescriptions often include three or more different herbs. Oftentimes, one herb is the main ingredient while the others act as its helpers. You've probably heard that many of the prescription drugs we take have been derived from herbs. The main difference is that the drugs use an isolated (often synthetic) compound while the herbs do not.

As is the case with any vitamin or drug, it's important to get the right combination, and the right amount. For the best—and safest—results, work with someone who knows herbal medicine.

Above all, be sure that you tell your physician that you're taking herbs and vitamins if you are taking any prescription medications or are scheduled to have surgery. A few herbs, for example, have been found to interfere with anesthesia, increase the risk of bleeding, and even lower blood pressure (which you obviously want to avoid **during** surgery). Some physicians recommend that you stop taking herbs and vitamins of any strength at least two weeks before surgery.

Arjuna. For hundreds of years, the bark of the Terminalia arjuna tree has been pulverized and used for heart conditions in India. In fact, it's now considered a well-proven cardiovascular "cure." Although it may be tempting to run out and find some arjuna if you have a heart condition, check with your physician first; it is a very powerful supplement.

As I mentioned earlier, vitamin E has proven in some clinical studies to be an effective supplement for controlling cholesterol levels. Arjuna's antioxidant capacity outperformed that of vitamin E in one randomized placebo-controlled trial in India. After only 30 days, the group taking arjuna decreased its average LDL-cholesterol levels by 25.6 percent while experiencing a 12.7 percent drop in total cholesterol. The groups that took either the placebo or 400 units of vitamin E had no significant change in either measurement.

Findings from other studies showed similarly positive outcomes for arjuna in connection with atherosclerosis, angina, and congestive heart failure (CHF). In fact, some doctors believe that the improvement it can bring about in cardiac-muscle functioning (along with subsequently improved pumping activity of the heart) is the primary benefit of this herb. The positive effects that arjuna has on the heart muscle appear to come from the *saponin glycosides* found in the herb, while compounds called *oligomeric proantho-*

cyanidins (OPCs) provide antioxidant benefits as well as vascular strengthening.

In another clinical trial, researchers gave arjuna to 15 stable angina sufferers for three months. The chest pain formerly experienced by these individuals dropped by 50 percent. Participants then took the herb before engaging in a treadmill test. Their exercise tolerance improved significantly. They still experienced angina symptoms, but they were delayed when the herb was ingested. Systolic blood-pressure levels of the arjuna-taking group also fell significantly, and tests showed that the HDL-cholesterol levels had increased.

Dried bark can be used daily in a dosage of 1 to 3 grams. Bark extract is often prescribed at 500 mg four times per day for CHF.

Artichoke extract. It has been almost 50 years since scientists first discovered that artichoke extract could reduce arterial plaque. Several more recent studies have reconfirmed that extract from the leaves of the wild artichoke plant can indeed reduce cholesterol and triglyceride levels. The extract appears to work in two ways. It breaks down the cholesterol and helps to eliminate it from the body through the liver, and it inhibits the production of cholesterol in the liver.

The power behind this herb can be found in the leaves, which contain a complex of biologically active compounds. Some researchers believe that one of the compounds, called *cynarin*, is the reason for its effectiveness, though others think it may be flavonoids or something else entirely. Nonetheless, when the leaves are dried, natural chemical changes take place to activate the cholesterol-lowering ability.

In one study, researchers gave either 1,800 mg of dried artichoke extract or a placebo to 143 people with cholesterol levels above 280. The study lasted six weeks. At its conclusion, those who took the extract had 18 percent lower total-cholesterol levels and 20 percent lower LDL levels. Other studies using artichoke extract have found drops in triglyceride levels.

As the study mentioned above demonstrates, fairly high levels of the extract may be required. A typical dosage recommendation is 300 mg to 640 mg three times a daily for at least six weeks or 1 to 4 grams of dried leaves three times a day. People who have any bile-duct obstructions (because of gallstones) should not take this herb.

Fenugreek. As is the case with the soybean and several other herbs discussed in this chapter, the seeds of this plant contain steroidal saponins—which may account for the benefits it provides to the heart. Fenugreek seeds also are rich in dietary fiber, which gives them another edge for heart health.

Several studies have found that fenugreek can help lower cholesterol and triglyceride levels in people with moderate atherosclerosis without lowering HDL-cholesterol levels.

For example, participants in a study conducted in India added 4 ounces a day of powdered fenugreek seeds to their diet for 20 days and "significantly" lowered their cholesterol levels. According to Daniel B. Mowrey, Ph.D., director of the American Phytotherapy Research Laboratory in Salt Lake City, "there's no question that fenugreek reduces cholesterol," and it may help people with diabetes as well.

Because fenugreek seeds taste bitter, many people prefer the powder form. Typically, 5 to 30 grams with each meal or 15 to 90 grams with one meal are recommended. Tinctures also may be taken, several times a day.

Ginkgo-biloba extract. You've probably heard that this herb, which is full of antioxidants, can help your memory and may even have potential for treating Alzheimer's disease. Lesser known is Ginkgo's reputation for fighting vascular disease. For a number of years now, in fact, Ginkgo biloba extract (GBE) has been prescribed (at least in Germany and France) for vascular diseases. Many studies have confirmed that it shows real promise for treating intermittent claudication, which is leg pain caused by obstructed blood flow (usually from atherosclerosis).

In fact, this is exactly what German researchers discovered in several different studies. In one 26-week clinical trial, more than 100 patients with peripheral arterial disease were divided into two groups. For two weeks, all took a placebo; then one group continued with the placebo and the other took one tablet of standardized GBE three times a day (120 mg total).

Researchers analyzed the results by comparing pain-free walking distance at the beginning of the trial with changes after eight, 16, and 24 weeks of treatment. After six months, the increase in pain-free walking distance in the GBE group was almost twice that of the placebo group. The GBE group reported no side effects. Other studies have found the same results with increases in pain-free walking up to 500 feet.

GBE gets its medicinal benefits from two active ingredients: *Ginkgo flavone glycosides* and *terpene lactones*. Labels on GBE bottles generally show that the product contains 24 percent of the first ingredient, which means that it contains a carefully measured balance of *bioflavonoids*. These are primarily responsible for GBE's antioxidant activity and its ability to reduce the stickiness of the platelets. This ability, in turn, improves the blood flow to the brain as well as the limbs, which, of course, helps prevent or treat heart disease and stroke. Six percent of the GBE should be *terpene lactone* components. These are associated with increased circulation to the brain and other parts of the body.

It is best to take an extract that is highly concentrated and comes from the leaves of the *Ginkgo biloba* tree. GBE is not fast-acting, though, and initial results often take about six weeks to appear; further results then continue to accumulate. By the time six months pass, you should see some truly significant results.

If it's the 50:1 extract you're taking, try taking 120 mg to 240 mg daily in two or three divided doses. Look to see whether the brand is standardized to 24 percent flavone glycosides and 6 percent terpene lactones, as is recommended. For a 1:5 tincture, take 2 mL to 4 mL three times a day. (Note that there is no well-established amount for the tincture and leaf varieties of *Ginkgo biloba*.)

Although it's generally considered safe, Ginkgo should be used with caution if another blood-thinning agent (such as warfarin or aspirin) is being used. Caution also should be exercised when taking it with natural blood thinners, such as garlic and high-dose vitamin E.

Grape-seed extract. This herb has at least two important functions. It contains flavonoids, which makes it an antioxidant (some say it's 50 times more powerful than vitamin E), and it helps to keep the arteries open.

More than 30 years ago, a French biochemist discovered that grape seeds also contain OPCs; these are antioxidants that improve blood circulation by reducing plaque in the vessels. (I mentioned OPCs before, under "Arjuna" on page 145.)

Grape-seed extracts can be found in fluid form, capsules, and tablets. Look for products that are standardized to 95 percent OPC content. As a preventative for arterial plaques, a dosage of 50 mg standardized extract per day is often recommended. For specific illness, doses of up to 300 mg per day have been recommended, but work with your doctor, nutritionist, or herbalist to determine the proper dosage for you and don't self-prescribe.

Grapefruit pectin. Way back in the 1970s, Dr. James Cerda, a gastroenterologist at University Hospital in Gainesville, Florida, started experimenting on reducing plaque build-up in the arteries of animals with various types of food fibers. He used pigs as his test subjects because they have a circulatory system similar to that of humans.

The pigs received a diet containing 40 percent saturated fat, and within a year their cholesterol levels had risen twelvefold. During the following nine months, half of the pigs received bran-type fibers with their high-fat diet while the others got various fruit pectins. The scientists discovered that the plaque levels of animals fed grapefruit pectin dropped by as much as 60 percent—even though the pigs remained on a high-fat diet. Human trials showed similar results. In one study, patients found their LDL was lowered by 11 percent—even if they made no other changes to their lifestyle or diet.

A report in the health journal *Clinical Cardiology* reached the following conclusion: "This study has shown that daily dietary supplementation of 15 grams of grapefruit pectin significantly lowered plasma cholesterol and improves the ratio of LDLC to HDLC in patients who are unable or unwilling to follow a low-risk diet."

Another study, of more than 200 patients, showed that pectin can lower LDL cholesterol between 25 percent and 30 percent in just four weeks. And for those willing to make dietary and lifestyle changes, such as exercising regularly and avoiding high-cholesterol foods, the results have been even better.

Few of us are likely to eat two grapefruits, rinds and all, per day—the amount needed to get therapeutic results. So, Dr. Cerda and his team mixed citrus pectin and guar gum with egg whites or soy to make the substance more palatable and easier to digest. This formula, later named ProFibe, can be mixed with beverages or food. Dr. Cerda says it's "as good as, if not better than, any prescription cholesterol-lowering medication now on the market." (See Appendix I for information on how to order ProFibe.)

Green tea. As I mentioned in the previous chapter, green tea is thought by many to be a real overall winner for the cardiovascular system. Although green, black, and oolong teas come from the same plant, green tea is the only one that's not fermented, so the active ingredients remain. Among the most valuable of those active ingredients are the *polyphenols*—perhaps *the* secret to green tea's benefits. Some researchers claim that GTPs (green-tea polyphenols) are even better antioxidants than vitamins C and E. Like a couple of the other herbs I've mentioned, green tea also contains OPCs.

The primary benefit of green tea is that it lowers cholesterol levels slightly. It also may make platelets in the blood less sticky. The jury's still out on whether it protects against atherosclerosis, but there is evidence that hints at this possibility as well.

Much of the research that has been done has been based on the amount of green tea typically consumed in Asian countries—about three cups per day (enough to provide around 240 mg to 320 mg of polyphenols). However, other researchers suggest that we may need as much as 10 cups per day to obtain the benefits! This is where supplements come in handy.

You can find tablets and capsules that contain the standardized extracts of GTP. Some provide up to 97 percent polyphenol content, which is equivalent to drinking 5 to 10 cups of tea.

Others include a standardized extract made of 80 percent total polyphenols and 55 percent epigallocatechin (the other ingredient). Generally, doses of 300 mg to 400 mg per day are considered appropriate.

Those who are adversely affected by caffeine should consider taking a decaffeinated version. If you are taking any blood-thinning medications, warfarin for example, you should check with your doctor before deciding to take a green-tea supplement. Green tea contains vitamin K, which can diminish the effect of warfarin and similar drugs.

Guggul gum. There's growing evidence that this gummy resin, which comes from the Indian mukul myrrh tree, can lower LDL-cholesterol and triglyceride levels as well as raise HDL levels. The gum has a long history of medicinal use in India, dating back thousands of years. The Indian government has even officially recognized the vast amount of evidence behind gugul's healing powers by approving a purified extract called guggulipid, which is now available worldwide.

The pure guggul gum used in the traditional medicine of India sometimes contained toxic compounds that could pose a danger to anyone taking it. However, the purified extract, guggulipid, has none of those toxic compounds and has been found to be as effective as some prescription drugs for lowering cholesterol and tryglyceride levels.

The reason for this success appears to be *guggulsterones*, compounds found in the resin. These sterones act as antioxidants and keep LDL cholesterol from spreading through the blood. Like many other successful heart herbs, guggul reduces the stickiness of platelets. In fact, according to one study, the extract works in a manner similar to at least one of the cholesterol-lowering drugs.

Clinical studies have consistently shown that guggul extracts do improve lipid levels in humans. One study comparing gugulipid to a common cholesterol-lowering prescription drug found that total cholesterol levels dropped 11% in the gugulipid group as compared to 10% in the prescription-drug group. In addition, almost two out of three of those taking gugulipid had their HDL-cholesterol levels increase, while none of those in the prescription, drug group experienced a change in their HDL levels.

In another study, 20 patients with high cholesterol were given 4.5 grams of gum guggul daily for 16 weeks while another 20 received a placebo. The researchers took blood samples at the beginning of the study and then every three weeks for three months. The cholesterol level of the guggul group dropped almost 22 percent after 16 weeks. Its triglyceride level dropped 27 percent. The HDL level increased by a whopping 35.8 percent!

The general dosage recommendation is 75 mg daily (three doses of 25 mg). Some experts, though, recommend dosages as high as 225 mg a day (usually split into two smaller daily doses). Most extracts contain 5 percent to 10 percent of the compound, and these can be safely taken for up to six months. The only real side effect reported are rashes and abdominal discomfort, but people with liver disease or inflammatory-bowel disease should use this herb with caution. It is important to note that although some supplements still have "guggul gum" listed among their ingredients, the toxic compounds sometimes found in the ancient forms of the gum are now safely removed from the resin.

Hawthorn for the heart. This common thorny shrub has been around since ancient times. More recently, it has truly become the darling of the heart world. Many consider it to be *the* herb for the heart, while, in truth, it is most valuable in treating people with congestive heart failure (CHF). That said, it also could help those with angina, atherosclerosis, hypertension, or some types of arrhythmia. Hawthorn is currently one of the most prescribed treatments for heart problems in Europe.

Hawthorn contains several *bioflavonoid*-type complexes, including OPCs, that act as potent antioxidants and appear to constitute the source of the plant's power. The active ingredients in the herbal extract dilate blood vessels, increase the heart's ability to pump, and improve the supply of energy to the heart. In other words, use of the herb results in more relaxed and open coronary blood vessels and a better-working heart muscle. Since the heart doesn't have to work as hard, the blood pressure stabilizes. This is how hawthorn relieves chest pain and reinforces a normal heartbeat.

Several clinical trials have proven that hawthorn is most helpful for people in the early stages of CHF. The findings of one study, in fact, showed that it is just as effective as the prescription drug captopril. A German study of 136 people with mild congestive heart failure compared hawthorn extract with a placebo. The group that took the extract had less shortness of breath and ankle swelling and was able to tolerate more exercise before angina occurred.

This herb comes in many forms: capsules, tinctures, standardized fluid and solid extracts, and even tea (though bitter). Capsules are usually recommended, because they offer the highest guarantee of potency.

Generally, standardized extracts contain 2.2 percent bioflavonoids or 18.75 percent OPCs. A common dosage recommendation is 80 mg to 300 mg of the extract in capsules or tablets two to three times per day. It takes about four to eight weeks before any improvements in blood pressure are seen.

If you remember nothing else about hawthorn, remember this: Although it is considered generally safe, hawthorn also is powerful. Work with a knowledgeable health-care provider if you have a heart problem and watch to see how your body reacts to the herb. If, for example, you experience more bouts of angina or become more exhausted while walking, stop taking the herb. You also should be cautious if you're taking any prescription medications, particularly those for the heart. Hawthorn may increase the action of some heart medications, so it is important to work with your doctor when deciding to try a hawthorn supplement. Improvements should be seen after six to eight weeks of treatment.

Red-yeast rice. For hundreds of years, Chinese practitioners have used this herb to treat a number of ailments, including poor blood circulation, such as experienced by people with intermittent claudication. It is made by growing red yeast, known as *Monascus purpureus*, on cooked nonglutinous rice. The resulting herb is actually a fermentation byproduct of this process.

About 20 years ago, researchers discovered that monacolin K, one of the ingredients in red-yeast rice, halts the enzyme in the liver (HMG-CoA reductase) that manufactures cholesterol in the body. For many years, this was very good news for those who wanted to fight cholesterol with herbs.

Clinical studies showed consistently high success rates for the use of red-yeast rice. For example, one study involved 187 people with mild to moderate elevations in cholesterol. With the use of red-yeast rice, their total cholesterol dropped more than 16 percent, their triglyceride levels dropped 24 percent, and their HDL increased 14 percent. In another study, with twice the number of participants, those rates came in as 22.7 percent, 31 percent, and 20 percent.

Unfortunately, in 1988, one of the most widely available red-yeast-rice products, Cholestin, ran into trouble. At the request of the patent-medicine giant Merck, the FDA began investigating Cholestin. It seems that it contained a natural phytochemical called mevinolin and that mevinolin is chemically identical to the patented cholesterol-lowering substance lovastatin, which can be found in Merck's drug Mevacor.

When the FDA discovered this fact, it declared Cholestin to be an unapproved drug and attempted to block its sale. The manufacturer of Cholestin sued the FDA and won but then lost on appeal. Thus, red-yeast-rice products are now difficult to find but not completely impossible to locate.

In spite of its proven effectiveness, there are some cautionary notes about red-yeast rice. First, it should never be used with other cholesterol-lowering drugs. Its similarity may enhance the effectiveness of the drug and increase the possibility of liver damage. Also, the chance of harmful side effects increases when red-yeast rice is taken with grapefruit products (this is also true of a number of prescription cholesterol drugs), so these, of course, should be avoided.

Although this varies, standardized extracts generally supply about 600 mg when taken two to four times a day. Many experts say that the most effective products come from the *Monascus purpureus* yeast. At least one researcher, however, says that the *Ruber purpureus* variety may contain the highest amount of natural Monacolin K, the active agent.

The Chelation Controversy

Chelation is an alternative therapy in which the chemical ethylenediaminetetraacentic (EDTA) is administered intravenously to someone suffering from cardiovascular problems. EDTA, developed in Germany in the 1930's for use in the dye industry, binds with minerals and metals including iron, mercury, copper, lead, zinc, aluminum and calcium. Medical researchers have found that the chemical is useful for treating those suffering from lead or arsenic poisoning. The chelating agents bind with the excess minerals in the body and then both the EDTA and the minerals are safely excreted in the urine. The chemical EDTA has been approved by the FDA for only this purpose.

A full course of chelation consists of twenty to thirty three-hour sessions. Proponents of the therapy say it is safer than traditional surgical procedures that are used to remove artery blockages. Practitioners who use chelation in their practices report that their patients show improvements in blood vessel blockages and exercise tolerance after this therapy.

There are numerous case reports and anecdotal reports in existence that speak positively for the use of chelation therapy. However, to date no conclusive clinical studies have been conducted to prove the benefits of the therapy. One study, conducted in 1994, in which atherosclerosis patients with blockages to the legs randomly received infusions of either chelating agents or an inactive saline solution resulted in a significant improvement the distance the patients could walk in both groups. No significant side effects were reported in either group. Another study, reported on in the Journal of the American Medical Association in January 2002, found no obvious benefits for use in the treatment of ischemic heart disease.

Choose Wisely

As you can see from reading this, there are a number of alternatives to prescription drugs for fighting heart disease. As I said at the beginning of this chapter, supplements like these, no matter how tempting, should always be used along with a balanced, low-fat diet and plenty of exercise. As you'll find out in the next chapter, on exercise, there are simply no shortcuts to a healthy heart.

CHAPTER 6

Exercise for a Healthy Heart

When it comes to the heart, exercise is just as important as a balanced, low-fat diet. Perhaps that is why the AHA has adopted its catchy exercise-campaign slogan: "Just move."

Unless you have a job in which you get brisk, sustained (uninterrupted), and regular aerobic exercise three to five times a week, "Just move" should become your mantra too. There's no way around it; to stay healthy, we all need to exercise.

In recent years, researchers worldwide have proven that a sedentary lifestyle—one that involves little or no physical activity—is a major risk factor for a growing list of chronic conditions, including heart disease and stroke. As you'll see below, studies have shown that, though it doesn't guarantee that you won't get heart disease, exercise reduces the risk—often significantly. It also helps out with several of the contributing risk factors, such as excess weight and diabetes.

Cardiovascular Fitness

As I said in the beginning of this book, the heart is a muscle. Like other muscles, it becomes bigger and stronger through exercise. The type of exercise required to strengthen the heart is called *aerobic*. Aerobic exercise involves the steady, continuous motion of the large muscles of the body. These activities depend on energy derived from oxygen consumption, and it is the cardiovascular system that meets these demands by pumping more blood to the muscles.

Achieving cardiovascular fitness requires a commitment. To make any progress, you must perform aerobic activities like those listed in the table below at least three or four times a week for 30 to 60 minutes at 50 percent to 80 percent of your heart's maximum capacity. (See page 168 under "Your Target Heart Rate.") However, some studies have found that even short bouts of exercise (10 minutes each) equaling at least 30 minutes may be just

GOLD-STAR EXERCISES FOR THE HEART

Here are some examples of the kinds of physical activities that can help your heart. There are others just as beneficial—if you do them vigorously enough and for at least 30 minutes.

bicycling	brisk walking
climbing stairs	cross-country skiing
jogging	jumping rope
roller-skating	rowing
running or jogging	swimming
uphill hiking	water aerobics
rebounding	kick boxing
racquetball or handball	

as beneficial as a continuous workout.

The term "intensity level" is often connected with aerobic exercise, and this refers to how hard your heart muscle is working. The level of intensity can be low, moderate, or high (vigorous). If you haven't been physically active, for example, you will start your exercise program with *low-intensity* physical activities. When done on a regular basis, even this type of activity helps lower the risk of heart disease. Strolling at one mile per hour and cycling on a level surface at five miles per hour are two examples of low-intensity activity.

More intensive exercise levels help your heart even more. *Medium- or moderate-intensity* exercise can include such activities as walking 3.5 miles per hour, cycling eight miles in one hour, and raking leaves for 30 minutes. To move your activity level up another notch to high-intensity exercise, you would have to jog five miles in an hour or cycle 12 miles in an hour.

No matter what type or level of exercise you perform, be sure to start with a five- to 10-minute warm-up. A warm-up can include slow walking or jogging, knee lifts, arm circles, or trunk rotations. At the end of your exercise routine, allow yourself another five or 10 minutes to cool down. Depending on the exercise you've done, slow walking or perhaps stretching might work. The warm-up and cooling-down periods give your heart the chance to make a more gradual transition.

Basking in the Benefits

As you may already know, developing a stronger cardiovascular system provides many heart-related benefits. It lowers your chances of having a heart attack, for example, and if you've already had one, it improves your chances of survival. In a continuing study of Harvard University alumni, researchers found that men who burn at least 2,000 calories a week walking or doing other moderate exercise have a 24 percent lower death rate from cardiac problems than those who do little or no exercise.

Even those who have already had one heart attack can reduce their chances of having another one by incorporating brisk activity into their schedules. The medical journal *Circulation* recently published a study about heart-attack survivors. The researchers found that those who increased their activity levels were 90 percent more likely than inactive patients to be alive in seven years!

Studies focused on women have shown similarly positive results from exercise. For example, a study published in the *New England Journal of Medicine* in 1999 suggested that women who walk at a moderate pace for three hours or more a week can cut their risks of both stroke and heart attack by one-third.

In Norway, researchers studied more than 14,000 women and found that those who exercise four to five times a week have a 50 percent lower chance of dying from stroke than those who only exercise once a week. Researchers also found that this level of exercise reduces stroke risk factors, such as blood-vessel disease, high cholesterol, obesity, and diabetes.

In terms of whether exercise will help you to avoid a stroke directly, scientists still aren't sure. The American Stroke Association (ASA) says no one's found a direct link yet. What is know, of course, is that exercising reduces the risk of heart disease, strokes, and other health problems. It's a safe bet that helping to prevent a heart attack through exercise may reduce the risk of some kinds of embolic strokes as well.

Aerobic activity improves the condition and functioning of the blood vessels. As mentioned above, the heart becomes stronger from aerobic exercise. It pumps more blood and oxygen to the body but doesn't have to work as hard to do it. Aerobic activity has a number of other positive effects on the blood vessels.

- Circulation improves, which helps keep the blood vessels clear of blood clots and plaque build-up and even reverses the process of hardening of the arteries (atherosclerosis).

- The *pulse rate* decreases. (See page 167 for more on the pulse rate.)

- It stimulates *angiogenesis*, which is the body's natural process of creating tiny new blood vessels to bypass clogged or diseased ones.

- It increases the level of HDLs, which protect the heart, and decreases the level of LDLs, which harm the heart.

Exercise prevents and helps to manage high blood pressure. The ability of exercise to reduce high blood pressure may be one of its biggest advantages. As you'll remember from earlier, high blood pressure is one of the major risk factors and a symptom of heart disease. Being able to reduce your blood pressure means you're reducing your risk of heart disease.

According to the findings of a study published in the February 2002 issue of *Preventive Medicine*, people who exercise moderately to vigorously at least five times a week are 25 percent less likely to have hypertension than their peers who get no exercise. Another study, done at the University of Pittsburgh's Graduate School of Public Health, found that exercise actually helps to stretch the arteries.

Blood vessels get naturally stiff as we age, and this causes our blood pressure to rise. Stiff arteries also can lead to a condition called *isolated systolic hypertension*, which means that just the top number of the blood-pressure reading is abnormally high. Systolic hypertension has been linked to an increased risk of a stroke or heart attack.

The University of Pittsburgh researchers evaluated more than 350 people ages 70 to 96 and discovered that those who were physically active had more flexible arteries. The arteries of people who exercised less were stiffer, and their resting heart rates were higher. Lead investigator Rachel Mackey said, "We saw people who had much younger arteries relative to their chronological age."

In addition to these heart-related benefits, here are a few more reasons to exercise:

- **Control your weight.** Exercising increases your body's metabolism, which burns calories. It helps build muscle tissue, which also burns more calories. A lower weight is good for your heart.

- **Improve your attitude.** A good workout releases *endorphins*, natural mood-elevating brain chemicals. A recent study showed that walking is more effective than taking tranquilizers for relieving anxiety. As you'll see below, under "Managing Stress", this contributes to a healthier heart.

- **Increase your energy.** Instead of eating a candy bar when you need a quick burst of energy, try taking a 10-minute walk. Dr. Robert Mayer, a professor at California State University, headed a study that found that a walk as short as 10 minutes not only produces extra energy but also produces a sudden burst of energy that outlasts the "power boost" of a candy bar. Fewer candy bars also mean fewer empty calories.

Long-term heart expert Dr. Denton A. Cooley—president, surgeon-in-chief, and founder of the Texas Heart Institute in Houston—confirms the benefits of exercise. "Among the best things we can do for ourselves are to fuel our body with low-fat food and exercise regularly. ... It's almost too simple. The foods we eat and our activity level directly influence our heart health. By beginning a weight-loss and exercise program, we may postpone or prevent heart disease."

Getting Started

For sedentary people, the biggest hurdle to exercising is usually taking the first step. But even before you take that step, look at the questions below. Do you have to answer "yes" to any of them? If so, you may want to consult with your doctor first about your desire to start a regular exercise program. You doctor might suggest that you take an exercise-stress test first to measure your heart rate and gage your reaction to exercise in a controlled surrounding.

- Do you smoke?

- Are you overweight?

- Has it been a long time since you exercised regularly?

- Have you ever had a heart attack? Do you have any other type of heart condition?

- Do you have a family history of early stroke or heart-attack deaths?

- What about problems with bones, joints, muscles, ligaments, or tendons?

- Do you have any medical conditions or other physical reasons for having exercise restricted?

- Are you taking any prescription drugs, especially any for blood pressure or other heart conditions?

- Do you have high blood pressure but don't take medication for it?

- Do you have insulin-dependent diabetes?

- Has your physician recommended that you perform only activities supervised by medical personnel?

- Do you feel any pain or pressure in the left side of your upper body (chest, neck, arm, and shoulder) when you are physically active?

- Have you had any chest pain during the last month or two?

- Do you ever lose consciousness or become dizzy?

- Are you excessively out of breath after just mild physical activity?

Did you answer "no" to the above questions? Great news! Before you put on your tennis shoes and get started, though, don't ignore these signs of possible heart problems:

- feeling pain or pressure in your chest, specifically on the left side or middle of it, as well as the left side of your neck and your left shoulder or arm

- experiencing feelings of sudden lightheadedness, breaking out in a cold sweat, having pale skin, or fainting

Choosing the "Right" Exercise

As the chart on page 159 suggests, there are many aerobic exercises from which you can choose. A number of people choose walking and later jogging or running, because those activities don't require much except working legs and a good pair of tennis shoes. However jogging or running can be stressful on some people's joints. Swimming is a good alternative activity for many people, because it's low-impact and, therefore, easier on the joints.

If you can't decide what from of exercise you want to do, here are a few points to consider:

- Do you want to exercise alone or with other people? Although companionship may motivate you, don't put off exercising while you find the right partner or class. Get going right away with another activity, such as walking, while you're looking for an activity with a group or partner.

- Would you rather exercise outdoors or indoors? Although indoor activities, such as stationary cycling, may be more convenient, walking outdoors may be more enjoyable. It's an individual choice, and the main point really is to choose an exercise that you'll want to continue.

- How much money do you want to spend? If you have a little extra, maybe a gym will help you get on the right track. If you don't, try walking outdoors or check on less-expensive community activities or facilities.

- What's the best time for you to exercise? Consider your daily life and decide whether your best exercise time is in the morning, afternoon or at night. Include exercise as a regular part of your routine.

Start out gradually and at a low level of intensity. Each time you exercise, increase the length of time a little. Don't be discouraged if you don't see results right away. It takes time to get in shape or back in shape, but, as the study described below shows, persistence and patience really do pay off.

Researchers from the Institute for Exercise and Environmental Medicine at Presbyterian Hospital in Dallas studied the effects of age and physical activity on the heart. Men in their early 50s participated in a training program that included walking, jogging, or cycling. By the end of the six months, the study participants were exercising about 4.5 hours a week.

According to the published report, a six-month endurance-training program of moderate intensity reversed a 30-year decline in cardiovascular fitness that normally occurs in middle age. Researchers said members of the group returned to the level of aerobic ability they had in their early 20s!

"The studies indicate that middle-aged men can actually reverse many of the negative results of not exercising, even after being physically inactive for a long time," said Dr. Benjamin Levine, study co-author and medical director of the Institute.

On the Pulse

You can track changes in your cardiovascular functioning by measuring your *pulse rate*, which is the number of times your heart beats per minute. It's a simple thing to take your pulse, and, when you first begin, it should be done before, during, and after an aerobic activity. For those who don't already know how to do it, here are a few quick instructions.

- The two best places to get your pulse rate are at the blood vessels on the left and right side of your neck (called the *carotid pulse* because these are the carotid arteries) and on the inside of your wrist below the base of the thumb (*radial pulse*).

- Place the tips of your first two fingers lightly over the blood vessel.

- Using a watch or clock with a second hand, count the beats of your heart for 10 seconds. Multiply that number by six, and that is your resting pulse rate for one minute.

A normal, resting heart rate is approximately 70 beats per minute. A well-conditioned heart can actually beat as few as 40 to 50 times a minute when at rest. It doesn't take a math whiz to see that a well-conditioned heart conserves energy. More importantly, this means that the heart is supplying oxygen-rich blood to the rest of the body with half the effort.

Cardiovascular or aerobic exercise will obviously increase your pulse above its normal resting rate, which is indeed the goal. The more intense the activity, the higher the rate will be. When you stop exercising, your pulse does not immediately return to normal but will do so gradually. The greater your level of fitness, the faster your pulse rate falls to its resting rate.

Your Target Heart Rate

Taking your pulse is widely accepted as a good method for measuring intensity during aerobic activities. Exercise that doesn't raise your heart rate to a certain level and keep it there for 20 minutes won't contribute significantly to cardiovascular fitness.

What you want to maintain is your *target heart rate (THR).* When you exercise, you will need to stay within a range (from a minimum to a maximum pulse rate) to get the benefits you need for your heart. You should use your THR as a guideline to help measure your fitness level before you start an exercise program and help track your progress afterward.

Most heart experts agree that the best aerobic level is a range that falls between 50 percent and 75 percent of a person's maximum heart rate. You can figure out your THR by doing the simple math problem shown below.

■ **Subtract your age from 220 to get your maximum heart rate [MHR].** If, for example, if you are 50, your MHR is 170. If you are 55, your MHR is 165. If you are 60, your MHR is 160. You get the picture. No matter what your age, just subtract it from 220.

■ **Multiply your MHR by .50 (or 50 percent).** This gives you the lowest point of your THR range. If, for example, you are 50, your lowest pulse rate should be 85. If you are 55, it should be 83. If you are 60, it should be 80. No matter what your MHR, just multiply it by .50 to get the lowest point of your range.

■ **Multiply your MHR by .75 (or 75 percent).** This gives you the highest point of the THR range. If, for example, if you are 50, your MHR is 127. If you are 55, your MHR is 123. If you are 60, your MHR is 120. No matter what your age, just multiply it by .75 to get your higher THR.

While exercising, you should keep your pulse between the lowest and highest numbers (which is your THR range). If you are 60, your THR range is between 80 and 120 beats per minute. If you are exercising at low intensity, which you should be if you're just starting, it should be at the lower end, and if you are exercising at high intensity, it should be at the higher end.

While exercising, take your pulse rate occasionally to make sure you're staying within the appropriate range for your age. Take a stopwatch or a watch with a second hand with you while you walk, for example, so that you can check this halfway through the allotted time. After several months, you can increase your maximum heart rate if you aren't feeling challenged.

Once you've stopped exercising and are sitting quietly, check your heart rate again after five minutes. This is your resting pulse rate.

Note that some medications, such as beta-blockers and those prescribed for hypertension, may skew the numbers determined for the THR range. If you are on any medications, particularly those mentioned, check in with your physician.

Just Walk

There are numerous reasons why many people choose to walk for cardiovascular fitness. For starters, walking really does improve the efficiency of one's heart, lowers his blood pressure and helps him lose weight. Walkers report very few injuries, and walking has the lowest dropout rate among all forms of exercise.

According to a report issued by the President's Council on Physical Fitness and Sports, walking is the only exercise in which the rate of participation does not decline in the participants' middle and later years. In a national survey, the highest percentage of regular walkers (39.4 percent) for any group was found among men 65 years of age and older.

Many fitness studies have shown that walking is, in fact, just as effective as running and other activities. For example, walking burns *about* the same number of calories per mile as jogging does. Brisk walking for one mile in 15 minutes is about the same as jogging for one mile in 8.5 minutes.

In weight-bearing activities like walking, heavier individuals will burn more calories than lighter people will. For example, studies show that a 110-pound person burns half as many calories as a 216-pound person walking at the same pace for the same distance.

When looking at the benefits to heart/lung endurance, how much you improve depends on your initial fitness level. Someone starting out in poor shape will benefit from a slow speed of walking, whereas someone in better condition would need to walk faster and/or farther to improve.

It doesn't take much to make a walk a workout. In fact, it's just a matter of pace and distance. Sauntering, strolling, and shuffling are not workouts. Moving at a "brisk" pace—one that makes your heart beat faster and causes you to breathe deeper—is a workout, however. The "talk test" can help you find the right pace. If you can carry on a conversation while walking, that's the right pace. If not, slow down a little.

The President's Council on Physical Fitness and Sports gives the following tips for beginning walkers.

- Hold your head erect, keeping your back straight and your abdomen flat. Point your toes straight ahead and swing your arms loosely at your sides.

- Land on the heel of the foot and roll forward to

drive off the ball of the foot.

- Take long, easy strides, but don't strain for distance. When walking up or down hills, or at a very rapid pace, lean slightly forward.

- Breathe deeply (keeping your mouth open if you need to).

Walking Journals

Some people find that keeping a regular log of their walking activity helps them to stick to their commitment and plot their progress. If you feel you would benefit from such a discipline, you may photocopy the *Walking Journal* blank form on pages 196-197 in Appendix I. After every walk, record the details of your walk on a form and keep your log in a folder. This form can also be adapted and used for other forms of aerobic exercise.

When you first begin your walking program, limit yourself to a comfortable distance and speed. Although this is an individual decision, I've included an exercise plan below that might work for you. At the least, it will give you a foundation that you can adapt to your own abilities. Increase your walking speed, distance, and number of walking sessions, as you get better at it.

Walk This Way: a Plan for Aerobic Fitness

The table on page 173 shows how your exercise plan might look. However, as I have mentioned already, it should fit your individual fitness level. If you haven't been off the couch in 20 years, you might want to reduce the minutes of exercise by half. If you're not totally sedentary, you might want to start out in week four.

Week Number	Warm up for...	Walk briskly for at least ...	Cool down for ...
1	5 minutes	5 minutes	5 minutes
2	5 minutes	8 minutes	5 minutes
3	5 minutes	11 minutes	5 minutes
4	5 minutes	14 minutes	5 minutes
5	5 minutes	17 minutes	5 minutes
6	5 minutes	21 minutes	5 minutes
7	5 minutes	25 minutes	5 minutes
8	5 minutes	28 minutes	5 minutes
9	5 minutes	30 minutes	5 minutes
10	5 minutes	33 minutes	5 minutes
11	5 minutes	37 minutes	5 minutes
12	5 minutes	40 minutes	5 minutes

A Plan to Move Toward Jogging

After a few months of following a regular walking plan, you might decide you want to increase the intensity of your exercise. An example of how that exercise plan might look is on page 174. You'll see that you'll alternate between walking and jogging for the first six weeks and that the time spent jogging will increase slightly each week. After a few weeks, you'll start out with walking but then jog for a longer time. The sample on the next page only goes to 20 minutes. If it works for you, however, you can design your own plan so you'll reach at least 30 minutes of jogging. Remember: This is something you'll do three times a week.

Week Number	Warm Up	Walk and Jog	Cool Down
1	Walk 5 minutes; then stretch a little.	**For 12 minutes total,** alternate walking briskly for one minute followed by jogging 5 minutes.	Walk 5 minutes; then stretch a little.
2	Walk 5 minutes; then stretch a little.	**For 16 minutes total,** alternate walking briskly for 5 minutes with jogging for 3 minutes.	Walk 5 minutes; then stretch a little.
3	Walk 5 minutes; then stretch a little.	**For 18 minutes total,** alternate walking briskly for 4 minutes with jogging for 5 minutes.	Walk 5 minutes; then stretch a little.
4	Walk 5 minutes; then stretch a little.	**For 20 minutes total,** alternate walking briskly for 4 minutes with jogging for 6 minutes.	Walk 5 minutes; then stretch a little.
5	Walk 5 minutes; then stretch a little.	**For 22 minutes total,** alternate walking briskly for 4 minutes with jogging for 8 minutes.	Walk 5 minutes; then stretch a little.
6	Walk 5 minutes; then stretch a little.	**For 26 minutes total,** alternate walking briskly for 4 minutes with jogging for 9 minutes.	Walk 5 minutes; then stretch a little.
7	Walk 5 minutes; then stretch a little.	**For 17 minutes total,** alternate walking briskly for 4 minutes with jogging for 13 minutes.	Walk 5 minutes; then stretch a little.
8	Walk 5 minutes; then stretch a little.	**For 20 minutes total,** alternate walking briskly for 5 minutes with jogging for 15 minutes.	Walk 5 minutes; then stretch a little.

Source: American Heart Association

Try Rebounding

There's another activity that you might not even think of as exercise because it is simply too much fun. It's called *rebounding*, it's excellent for your heart-health, and it's performed on a small trampoline (sometimes called a rebounder). Rebounders are almost identical to the original trampoline invented in the late 1930s. The small rebounder started appearing in the 1970s; since then, it has provided an effective—and fun—way to exercise.

Studies by NASA and the U.S. Air Force found that exercising on the rebounder is 68 percent more effective than jogging when it comes to reducing fat and improving overall fitness levels, particularly cardiopulmonary fitness. One unique thing about this small trampoline is that it provides the benefits of walking and jogging without the impact. The firm "bounce-back" of the polypropylene mat builds endurance levels and lower-body muscles but pampers joints and tendons. You can get the aerobic exercise your heart needs without stressing your joints!

The rebounding exercise increases your aerobic capacity, builds the strength of your heart muscle, and, in fact, infuses energy into all of your body cells. Rebounding quickly gets your blood moving and keeps your heart muscle pumping. You'll reach your target heart rate in no time and stay there as long as you need to do so.

Studies have found that almost twice as many people continue an exercise program of rebounding than continue a jogging regimen after one year. A yearlong study of various forms of exercise showed that 58 percent of participants who performed rebounding were still doing it after one year. This is a very high success rate for aerobic exercise! If you decide that rebounding is the path you want to take to aerobic fitness, consider, for safety's sake, buying a rebounder that includes handrails. Here are a few other practice tips:

- If you have been inactive for some time, or if you exercise only once or twice per week, you should start slowly.

- Get acquainted with the feel of the rebounder. Start out slowly by rolling your feet in a heel-toe motion while keeping them on the mat. Until you get your balance, keep in touch with the handrails. Then let go and try swinging your arms to mimic the arm motion used in running. Don't get carried away with arm swinging though, because too much may actually hurt your back. This action will help your coordination and improve your upper-body-muscle tone.

- Once you're familiar with the rebounder and adequately warmed up, you can rebound stiff-legged—allowing your body to just come off the surface. Soon, you will feel a pumping effect in your muscles. Tightening your upper-body muscles (isometric contraction) will help exercise your entire body.

- At first, exercise every other day. Try to rebound for five minutes and then rest. Build up to 15 minutes over the next two weeks or so.

- Once you're comfortable, you may start exercising more vigorously and more often. For example, increase your pace and lift your legs to imitate running. Alternate three minutes at a fast pace with three minutes at a slow pace. Rest three minutes between a couple of alternating sets.

■ Set a goal to rebound five times per week.

■ After a few months, incorporate stiff-legged, lowheight bounding. A slight bend in the knees is necessary to bound off the mat. This exercise will help your muscular development and your overall body strength.

Opt for Movement—Any Movement

While it's true that a focus on aerobic exercise is a priority for a healthy heart, two other categories of exercise should be considered for true overall fitness. These are known as *anerobic,* because they have no cardiovascular benefits.

Strength-building exercises like weightlifting make your muscles and bones stronger and increase your metabolism, which should help you lose weight if that's your goal.

Flexibility exercises, such as doing yoga or perhaps stretching as a warm-up to aerobic activity, help tone your muscles and can improve and even prevent some muscle and joint problems.

Don't restrict yourself to only your formal exercise time or activities. Instead, think of all the ways you can incorporate movement into your everyday life. Here are some examples, but I'm sure you can think of many more.

■ Rake leaves instead of using a leaf blower.

■ Walk or bicycle two blocks to the corner store instead of driving.

- Park farther away at the shopping mall or grocery store so you can walk the extra distance.

- Take the stairs instead of the elevator in office buildings.

- Walk instead of using a cart when you're golfing.

You get the picture—just move! Every little bit helps.

Losing Weight

Although this chapter isn't specifically about losing weight, being overweight is a contributing risk factor for heart disease. If you fall into this category, here are a few exercise guidelines that might help.

The key to weight control is keeping food and physical activity in balance. When you consume only as many calories as your body needs, your weight will usually remain constant. If you take in more calories than your body needs, you will put on excess fat. If you expend more energy than you take in, you will burn excess fat.

To lose 1 pound, a person has to burn off 3,500 calories. This can be accomplished in one of two ways.

- Exercise more but consume the same number of calories. According to the American Heart Association, a 200-pound person who consumes the same number of calories but walks briskly every day for 1.5 miles will lose about 14 pounds in one year.

- Exercise more but eat fewer calories—the ultimate way to lose weight.

Exercise plays an important role in weight control. When we perform more physical activity, we call on stored calories for extra fuel. Recent studies show that exercise not only increases your metabolism during a workout but also causes your metabolism to stay increased for a period of time after you exercise, allowing you to burn more calories. How much exercise is needed to make a difference in your weight depends on the amount and type of activity and how much you eat. Aerobic exercise burns fat.

A medium-sized adult would have to walk more than 30 miles to burn up 3,500 calories, the equivalent of 1 pound of fat. Although that may seem like a lot, you don't have to walk the 30 miles all at once. Walking a mile a day for 30 days will achieve the same result, as long as you don't increase the amount of food you eat to negate the effects.

If you consume 10 calories a day more than your body needs, you will gain approximately 10 pounds in a year. You can take that weight off, or keep it off, by doing 30 minutes of moderate exercise daily. The combination of exercise and diet offers the most flexible and effective approach to weight control.

Lack of physical activity causes muscles to get soft. Once-active people who continue to eat as they always have after settling into sedentary lifestyles tend to suffer from "creeping obesity."

The more vigorous your exercise, of course, the more calories you burn. If you walked three miles in one hour, for example, you would burn approximately 320 calories. If you ran 10 miles in an hour, you would burn almost 1,300 calories. Bicycling six miles for an hour burns about 250 calories. (These are only averages, though, and the calories you really burn up depend upon your individual weight.)

Managing Stress

Maybe you're one of the lucky ones who experience no stress in life and therefore don't have to worry about managing it. But for the other 99.9 percent of us, stress, both the positive and negative kind, is a fact of life. The results of numerous studies suggest that adding stress management to routine heart-disease treatment might lessen some patients' long-term risk of complications.

Consider, for example, research that Dr. James A. Blumenthal of Duke University in Durham, North Carolina, and his colleagues conducted. For five years, they studied 94 men with heart disease. The participants who were part of the stress-management group attended 16 small-group sessions where they learned ways to control negative emotions and thoughts, techniques for muscle relaxation, and other stress-calming tactics. The benefits that the stress-management group received were clear.

- They had fewer heart procedures than did those in the control group.

- Few of the 94 men in the study had a heart attack, and only one died. But in the study's first year, two men who received only standard care (i.e., no stress-management training) had a heart attack while none in the stress-reduction group did.

- Patients in the stress-reduction group had lower hospitalization and physicians' costs over five years than did men in the standard-care group.

"These findings confirm the added value of stress management training to usual medical care, and indicate that such training is associated with fewer adverse cardiac events and less medical expenditures," Blumenthal wrote in the Jan. 15, 2002, *American*

Journal of Cardiology.

Many other studies on stress management have been performed using patients who have hypertension. The National Heart, Lung, and Blood Institute issued a report that included a summary of the findings of 25 randomized, controlled clinical trials of stress management in hypertensive patients. In 12 of the 25 trials, those assigned to the stress-management group experienced a greater reduction in BP than their counterparts in the control group. Beneficial results were reported both from studies conducted in the workplace and in clinical settings, according to the NHLBI report.

Ohio State University researchers conducted studies of a different sort. Their research shed light on how stress can lead to heart damage when they found that short periods of psychological stress can slow down the body's ability to clear triglycerides— heart-damaging fats—from the blood. They compared the results to those of a session in which the volunteers rested. They found that in all cases, stress caused triglycerides to stay in the bloodstream longer. The bottom line, according to this research, is that people don't metabolize fats as rapidly and efficiently during periods of stress. What this means in practical terms is that if you tend to reach for high-fat snack foods during times of stress that fat is going to end up circulating in your blood for a longer period of time than it would normally.

In a related study, the results of which were recently published in the *Journal of Behavioral Medicine*, investigators found that among the participants in their subject group of 103 healthy, middle-aged women, those who were prone to "angry outbursts" or hostility had measurably less-healthy cholesterol levels than did women in the same group who had calmer reactions and were able to control their hostility. The women who had poor anger control had higher total- and LDL-cholesterol levels.

It was once the case that when anyone spoke of a personality type that was more prone to heart disease than the average, he was referring to a "type A" personality. Typically, someone with a "type A" personality is a person who is very time-driven and competitive and often finds it difficult to relax. But at the 2001 annual meeting of the American Heart Association, a new type of personality, the "type D" personality, was being discussed. According to the Baltimore Epidemiologic Catchment Area Study, people who tend to be easily stressed, pessimistic, and negative thinkers (called "type D" personalities) are four more times more likely to suffer from heart attacks than are others. The relationship between depression and lower survival rates of patients suffering with heart disease was already a well-established fact. However, this study, along with a number of other European studies, is being said to clearly demonstrate that feelings of stress and worry over relatively small everyday events significantly increases your risk of a heart attack. The message is clear: *just relax!*

Techniques for Taming Tension

The expert opinion is clear: Learning how to relax and control negative stress can have a number of health benefits for you. But how do you begin to control the stress in your life? There are many ways for you to learn to tame that tension. Regular exercise, relaxation techniques, meditation, and biofeedback are all helpful for stress management.

One very successful program for reversing heart disease combined dietary restrictions, moderate exercise, and stress-management techniques on a daily basis.

The stress-management techniques used in the program included one hour a day of stretching, breathing, meditation (silent and guided) or prayer, progressive relaxation, and group support. These techniques, which are derived from yoga, are designed to increase and focus awareness, improve concentration, quiet the mind and body, and help people rediscover inner sources of well-being.

Most of us don't have the chance to participate in a formalized program such as this, but there are some simple things we can do for ourselves without the help of the experts.

First, learn to identify your own stress so you can decide how to cope with it. Be aware that the following may be symptoms of a stress-related illness: fatigue, insomnia, headaches, indigestion, irritability, muscle spasms, varied eating habits, and lack of concentration. Then design a soothing environment for yourself, one that offers silence and few outside distractions. When you go to this physical place, your only goal should be to consciously try to relax.

Pick up a book on, or take a class in, yoga or tai chi. These Eastern forms of movement have been around for a very long time, and their value has been proven over and over through scientific studies and practical experience. They improve strength and flexibility, and they also may be used to reduce stress levels. Although some "yoga postures" (a specific term for yoga exercises) can get complicated, many of the beginning ones are simple and gentle on the body. Tai chi is a gentle type of exercise that has been used by people in China for centuries, and it is the type of exercise that can be practiced by people who are well into old age.

When you need to relax, perform a few simple yoga postures and try the following relaxation techniques.

Deep breathing. You've probably noticed that when you get stressed, such as when you're angry, your breath becomes shallow and rapid. Taking a deep breath is almost an automatic response to enable you to calm down, and that's exactly what this relaxation focuses upon. Here are the basic steps.

- Count to 10 as you slowly and deeply inhale through your nose. Be sure that as you do this, your abdominal area, not your chest, rises.

- Count to 10 as you exhale through your nose—again slowly and completely.

- Focus completely on this breathing-and-counting cycle for five to 10 repetitions.

- Repeat this several times throughout the day, especially when you feel agitated or anxious.

Muscle relaxation. This exercise goes well with the deep-breathing practice described above. This resting pose is one of the most important in yoga. Called Savasana in Sanskrit, it translates into English as "corpse pose," which should give you some idea of just how relaxed your limbs should be when you assume the posture.

- Lie down on your back in a comfortable place and without crossing your limbs.

- Begin the deep-breathing exercise described above.

- Tense each muscle group for a count of 5 and then release the tension. Visualize the muscle group to be as heavy as lead. (Here's where the name "corpse pose" comes in.) Start with the muscles in your face and repeat this movement all the way down the body to the tips of your toes. Make sure you don't miss any part of your body.

- Imagine that you can perform this exercise on your internal organs as well. Tense and release each set of internal organs from top to bottom.

- Remember to focus on your breathing throughout this exercise.

Meditation. As you may know, meditation can be used as a religious practice or simply as a therapeutic technique for relaxation. The point is to quiet the mind or relax all thoughts. The benefits of meditation may at first seem farfetched. After all, all you're required to do is to sit quietly in an upright position with your eyes closed and relax. But the benefits will soon become clear. In fact, some medical researchers have found that practiced meditators can reduce their heart rates and lower their blood-pressure readings during a session.

Some individuals prefer to sit in a chair, while others sit on a pillow placed on the floor with their legs crossed. Once again, breathing is the only activity you perform. Here are a few tips to get you started.

- Pay close attention to the inhalation and exhalation of your breath. You might notice that your breathing will naturally elongate and your breath will sound calmer.

- Be aware that your mind will wander. Notice that this is happening and let the thoughts come and go. Always return to your breathing exercise.

- Instead of, or in addition to, performing the breathing exercise, you might want to try repeating a word that has a specific sound but no meaning (a mantra) over and over.

- Try to stay in the present moment. Concentrate on your breathing or repeat the mantra to do this.

Acupuncture. You might not be able to imagine how sticking little needles into strategic spots on your body could possibly be relaxing, but researchers are finding that it may be just that. It appears that acupuncture treatments work on the sympathetic nervous system, which is the part of the body that regulates involuntary movements like your heartbeat and blood pressure.

When we're afraid or anxious, this system goes on automatic pilot and forces the heart to deliver more blood to the parts of the body that need it. When people have heart failure, the system is always in panic mode; this means that the already weak heart must work even harder.

A study conducted at the University of California, Los Angeles (UCLA) showed that acupuncture actually reduced sympathetic-nervous-system activity. The researchers found that the treatment "significantly lowers stress and improves heart function in the very sickest heart-failure patients."

Dr. Holly Middlekauff, lead author of the report documenting the UCLA study, said, "Advanced heart-failure patients often have two or three times more sympathetic nerve activity than normal individuals. It has been shown that the greater this activity is, the worse the outlook for the patient—so reducing it could be crucial."

Although these researchers haven't officially recommended acupuncture as a treatment for stress, many practitioners, as well as individuals, do believe that it has a calming effect. Maybe it will work for you too.

Defying the Odds

Findings from a study conducted by Dr. Robert H. Glew and colleagues from the University of New Mexico in Albuquerque adds an interesting twist on the healthy-lifestyle prescription many of us have been trying to follow. It's "interesting" but not one I'm suggesting you try, although it does show just how important exercise (and perhaps the right genes!) can be.

Glew and his partners conducted a study of the Fulani of Nigeria, a nomadic African tribe. Despite their fatty diets (and high protein intake), members of the tribe had healthy cholesterol levels. The researchers attribute this fact to the population's high physical-activity level, relatively low calorie intake, and lack of smoking.

The research team took blood samples from 121 Fulani men and women ages 15 to 77 and measured the levels of total, low-density-lipoprotein (LDL), and high-density-lipoprotein (HDL) cholesterol; several vitamins; and homocysteine. In addition, they evaluated the group's nutrient intake.

Overall, men consumed more than 1,600 calories a day and women consumed close to 1,500. Nearly 50 percent of those calories came from fat (with half of those coming from saturated fat). Keep in mind that the AHA advises that we take in no more than 30 percent of our calories from fats and no more than 10 percent from saturated fat.

Despite their total disregard for the fatty foods eaten, participants' average levels of total cholesterol and HDL cholesterol came within the ranges recommended in our country. Their average LDL actually went below recommended levels. The average body mass index (BMI), a measure of weight and height, was about 20. A BMI of 25 or more is considered overweight.

In an *American Journal of Clinical Nutrition* article, Glew and colleagues wrote that "despite a diet high in saturated fat, Fulani adults have a lipid profile indicative of a low risk of cardiovascular disease." They added that, "this finding is likely due to their high activity level." They also pointed out that the current recommendations about the risk factors connected with heart disease resulted from studies conducted in Western nations, where the majority of individuals are relatively sedentary.

"Our...findings with the Fulani do not support the dogma of the past 50 years that high-fat diets necessarily raise cholesterol concentrations," the researchers conclude.

I conclude that, although fascinating, this is a very unique situation—one that most of us will never enjoy. Unfortunately, since our modern lifestyles encourage us to be sedentary, we must be vigilant in incorporating exercise and physical movement into our lives. Like a balanced, low-fat diet full of nutrition, physical activity is a change that requires a lifelong commitment.

The hardest part, as I've already said, will be getting started, and the next-hardest part will be staying committed. But when you start seeing results, you'll know that what may at first appear to be sacrifice is actually a blessing—and your heart will thank you for it by performing more efficiently. Good luck!

· A P P E N D I X I ·

Resources That Can Help

There's no reason to be in the dark about how to fight heart disease, because, in addition to what I've included in this book, there are many helpful resources out there to lend a hand. The Internet is by far the easiest to access and the least expensive. By using a common search engine like www.yahoo.com or www.google.com and typing in a search for "heart disease" (or something more specific, such as "high blood pressure"), you'll be pleasantly surprised by the wealth of information at your fingertips.

Below, I've included a few places where you can find up-to-date information on cardiovascular disease and on how to fight it.

GROUPS AND ORGANIZATIONS

AMERICAN ASSOCIATION FOR NATUROPATHIC PHYSICIANS (AANP)

3201 New Mexico Avenue, NW Suite 350
Washington, DC 20016
Phone: (202) 895-1392 or toll free (866) 538-2267
Email: member.services@Naturopathic.org
Website: www.naturopathic.org
This national professional society represents naturopathic

physicians who are licenses (eligible for licensing) as primary care providers. Referrals to a naturopath in your area are available through their website at www.naturopathic.org.

AMERICAN BOTANICAL COUNCIL

P.O. Box 144345
Austin, TX 78714-4345
Phone: (512) 926-4900
Fax: (512) 926-2345
Website: www.herbalgram.org

This nonprofit educational organization focuses on herbal medicine. The American Botanical Council (ABC) offers a wide variety of science-based and difficult-to-find resources on the subject. Its current catalog includes more than 300 books, monographs, special reports, and video-tapes, as well as computer software.

THE AMERICAN COLLEGE FOR ADVANCEMENT IN MEDICINE (ACAM)

23121 Verdugo Drive, Suite 204
Laguna Hills, CA 92653
Phone: (949) 583-7666 or (800) 532-3688
E-Mail: info@acam.org
Website: www.acam.org

This organization provides referrals to naturopathic physicians, who can guide you in using preventative/nutritional medicine, on their website at www.acam.org.

AMERICAN HEART ASSOCIATION

National Headquarters
7272 Greenville Ave.
Dallas, TX 75231
Phone: (800) 242-8721
Website: www.americanheart.org

The AHA is one of the leading authorities on heart disease and stroke in this country, and its Website is a treasure chest of information. Included is information on the following.

- warning signs of a heart attack or stroke
- diseases and conditions
- healthy lifestyle choices, including information on nutrition and vitamin supplements
- a heart and stroke encyclopedia
- various other publications and resources

THE AMERICAN HOLISTIC HEALTH ASSOCIATION

PO Box 17400
Anaheim, CA 92817-7400
Phone: (714) 779-6152
E-mail: mail@ahha
Website: www.ahha.com

This organization represents M.D.'s and D.O.'s who combine mainstream medicine and complimentary therapies in their practices. They offer several resources on their website at www.ahha.com for locating qualified holistic and alternative practitioners.

AMERICAN STROKE ASSOCIATION

National Headquarters
7272 Greenville Ave.
Dallas, TX 75231
Phone: (888) 478-7653
Website: www.strokeassociation.org

The American Stroke Association (ASA) is a division of the American Heart Association. It is strictly focused on research and ways to reduce disability and death from strokes. Its Website also contains useful information.

AMERICAN YOGA ASSOCIATION

PO Box 19986
Sarasota, FL 34276
Phone: (941) 927-4977
E-mail: info@americanyogaassociation.org
Website: www.americanyogaassociation.org

This not for profit organization provides high-quality instruction and educational resources to those who are interested in yoga. Creators of the "Easy Does it Yoga" program specially designed for seniors and the physically challenged. They offer general information about yoga and tips on choosing a yoga instructor on their website at www.americanyogaassociation.org.

THE NATIONAL HEART, LUNG, AND BLOOD INSTITUTE

(part of the National Institutes of Health)

Phone: (301) 592-8573
Fax: (301) 592-8563

Website: www.nhlbi.nih.gov

The NHLBI Health Information Center develops and maintains information on numerous topics related to the heart, lungs, and blood, including angina, high blood pressure, arrhythmia, heart attacks, and congestive heart failure. It provides materials for the National High Blood Pressure Education Program, the National Cholesterol Education Program, the National Heart Attack Alert Program, and other similar programs.

Public- and patient-education materials are available on numerous topics, including cholesterol, high blood pressure, heart disease, exercise, obesity, and strokes. You'll also find detailed information on the very successful DASH diet discussed in Chapter 4.

FURTHER READING

THE ANTIOXIDANT MIRACLE: PUT LIPOIC ACID, PYCOGENOL, AND VITAMINS E AND C TO WORK FOR YOU

Lester Packer and Carol Colman

The main author is a molecular-cell biologist, and this book, which reviewers call fairly technical, describes breakthroughs in antioxidant research. It also offers the "Packer plan"—a prescription of five antioxidants that join to fight diseases: vitamins C and E, glutathione, lipoic acid, and coenzyme Q_{10}. Packer describes the benefits and actions of these antioxidants and also recommends other flavonoid supplements, such as Ginkgo biloba and pycnogenol (made from the bark of pine trees); several carotenoids; and selenium. It also provides information on foods high in antioxidants.

THE ANTIOXIDANTS

by Richard A. Passwater

AND

ALL ABOUT ANTIOXIDANTS

also by Richard A. Passwater and edited by Jack Challem

Dr. Richard Passwater, one of the leading researchers in the world in antioxidants, began his experiments in 1970. These books provide information on how free radicals harm the body and how antioxidants help prevent that damage. Many reviewers have called those books great beginners' guides.

THE ARGININE SOLUTION

Drs. Robert Fried and Woodson C. Merrel

L-arginine is being touted as a "magic bullet" for the cardiovascular system. Evidence is building that it really does have extraordinary health benefits, and this book discusses how it helps to eliminate blockage and maintain blood flow.

THE RELAXATION RESPONSE

Dr. Herbert Benson, M.D., and Miriam Z. Klipper (contributor)

Here's an old classic that still offers valuable information for stress management, especially for people who know nothing about it. When it was published in 1975, it was considered groundbreaking. After conducting studies at Boston's Beth Israel Hospital and Harvard Medical School, Dr. Benson showed that certain relaxation techniques, such as meditation, provide enormous physical benefits by, for example, lowering blood pressure and reducing heart disease. The book includes guidelines for meditation among other things.

UNLEASHING THE POWER OF FOOD: RECIPES TO HEAL BY

Master FaXiang Hou

Master Hou, fifth-generation heir to one of China's most revered families of natural healing Masters, reveals his most-celebrated food cures in this important book of healing recipes. His methods, handed down from father to son for literally thousands of years, are shared with readers in an easy-to-read text with literally hundreds of curative recipes, including specific "prescriptions" for fighting heart disease and hypertension and achieving lasting weight loss. Master Hou explains the basic building blocks of Chinese medicine and drives home the point that *we are what we eat.*

WALKING JOURNAL

Date   /   /

PACE of walk	TIME PLANNED for walking (in minutes)	ACTUAL TIME walked (in minutes)	DISTANCE walked (in miles/blocks)

◇ Slow
◇ Moderate
◇ Brisk

COMMENTS
(route, weather, how you felt before/after)

Approximate
CALORIES BURNED

M Y   W A L K I N G   J O U R N A L

Date   /   /

PACE of walk	TIME PLANNED for walking (in minutes)	ACTUAL TIME walked (in minutes)	DISTANCE walked (in miles/blocks)

◇ Slow
◇ Moderate
◇ Brisk

COMMENTS
(route, weather, how you felt before/after)

Approximate
CALORIES BURNED

M Y   W A L K I N G   J O U R N A L

Date   /   /

PACE of walk	TIME PLANNED for walking (in minutes)	ACTUAL TIME walked (in minutes)	DISTANCE walked (in miles/blocks)

◇ Slow
◇ Moderate
◇ Brisk

COMMENTS
(route, weather, how you felt before/after)

Approximate
CALORIES BURNED

M Y   W A L K I N G   J O U R N A L

Recipes for Staying Young at Heart

As I discussed in Chapter 4 and mentioned throughout the book, diet plays one of the most important roles in heart health. If you're serious about doing something good for your heart, and your overall health, you might have to make some changes in the way you eat. The good news is that you don't have to give up taste. Instead of concentrating on what you're giving up by making some changes in your diet, think of what you'll gain in heart health!

The recipes below are samples from the National Heart, Lung, and Blood Institute's *Stay Young at Heart* recipe collection. You can find these and more delicious and healthy recipes on the NHLBI Website: www.nhlbi.nih.gov.

SOUPS

BEAN AND MACARONI SOUP

This cholesterol-free tasty dish is virtually fat-free and is prepared with only 1 tablespoon of oil for 16 servings.

2 cans (16 oz.) great northern beans
1 Tbsp olive oil
1/2 lb fresh mushrooms, sliced
1 cup onion, coarsely chopped
2 cups carrots, sliced
1 cup celery, coarsely chopped
1 clove garlic, minced
3 cups cut-up, peeled fresh tomatoes or 1 1/2 lbs canned whole tomatoes
1 tsp dried sage
1 tsp dried thyme
1 tsp dried oregano
1 tsp freshly ground black pepper
1 bay leaf, crumbled
4 cups cooked elbow macaroni

Drain beans and reserve liquid.
Rinse beans.
Heat oil in a 6-quart kettle; add mushrooms, onion, carrots, celery, and
    garlic and sauté for 5 minutes.
Add tomatoes, sage, thyme, oregano, pepper, and bay leaf.
Cover and cook over medium heat for 20 minutes.
Cook macaroni according to directions on package, using unsalted
    water. Drain when cooked. Do not overcook.
Combine reserved bean liquid with water to make 4 cups.
Add liquid, beans, and cooked macaroni to vegetable mixture.
Bring to a boil; cover and simmer until soup is thoroughly heated. Stir
    occasionally.

Yield: 16 servings; Serving size: 1 cup
Each serving provides the following:
Calories: 158 • Total fat: 1 g. • Saturated fat: less than 1 g.
Cholesterol: 0 mg • Sodium: 154 mg*

If you use canned tomatoes, sodium content will be higher.

CANNERY ROW SOUP

Using fish and clam juice makes this tasty soup heart-healthy.

2 lb varied fish fillets (haddock, perch, flounder, cod, sole, etc.), cut into 1-inch-square cubes
2 Tbsp olive oil
1 clove garlic, minced
3 carrots, cut in thin strips
2 cups celery, sliced
1/2 cup onion, chopped
1/4 cup green peppers, chopped
1 can (28 oz) whole tomatoes, cut up, with liquid
1 cup clam juice
1/4 tsp dried thyme, crushed
1/4 tsp dried basil, crushed
1/8 tsp black pepper
1/4 cup fresh parsley, minced

Heat oil in a large pan.
Sauté garlic, carrots, celery, onion, and green pepper in oil for 3 minutes.
Add all remaining ingredients except parsley and fish.
Cover and simmer for 10 to 15 minutes or until vegetables are fork-tender.
Add fish and parsley.
Simmer, covered, 5 to 10 minutes more or until fish flakes easily and is opaque.
Serve hot.

Yield: 8 servings
Serving size: 1 cup each
Each serving provides the following:
Calories: 170
Total fat: 5 g.
Saturated fat: less than 1 g.
Cholesterol: 56 mg
Sodium: 380 mg

MINESTRONE SOUP

A cholesterol-free classic Italian vegetable soup brimming with fiber-rich beans, peas, and carrots.

1/4 cup olive oil
1 clove garlic, minced, or 1/8 tsp. garlic powder
1 1/3 cups coarsely chopped onion
1 1/2 cups coarsely chopped celery and leaves
1 can (6 oz) tomato paste
1 Tbsp chopped fresh parsley
1 cup sliced carrots, fresh or frozen
4 3/4 cups shredded cabbage
1 can (1 lb) tomatoes, cut up
1 cup canned red kidney beans, drained and rinsed
1 1/2 cups frozen peas
1 1/2 cups fresh green beans
a dash of hot sauce
11 cups water
2 cups uncooked, broken spaghetti

Heat oil in a 4-quart saucepan.
Add garlic, onion, and celery and sauté for about 5 minutes.
Add all remaining ingredients except spaghetti and stir until the
   ingredients are well mixed.
Bring to a boil.
Reduce heat, cover, and simmer for about 45 minutes or until
   vegetables are tender.
Add uncooked spaghetti and simmer 2-3 minutes only.

Yield: 16 servings
Serving size: 1 cup
Each serving provides the following:
   Calories: 153
   Total fat: 4 g.
   Saturated fat: less than 1 g.
   Cholesterol: 0 mg
   Sodium: 191 mg

FISH ENTRÉE

MEDITERRANEAN BAKED FISH

*This dish is baked and flavored with a Mediterranean-style tomato,
onion, and garlic sauce to make it lower in fat and salt.*

2 tsp olive oil
1 large onion, sliced
1 can (16 oz.) whole tomatoes, drained (reserve juice) and coarsely
 chopped
1 bay leaf
1 clove garlic, minced
1 cup dry white wine
1/2 cup reserved tomato juice, from canned tomatoes
1/4 cup lemon juice
1/4 cup orange juice
1 Tbsp fresh grated orange peel
1 tsp fennel seeds, crushed
1/2 tsp dried oregano, crushed
1/2 tsp dried thyme, crushed
1/2 tsp dried basil, crushed
black pepper to taste
1 lb fish fillets (sole, flounder, or sea perch)

Heat oil in a large nonstick skillet. Add onion and sauté over moderate
 heat for 5 minutes or until soft.
Add all remaining ingredients except fish.
Stir well and simmer for 30 minutes, uncovered.
Arrange fish in 10-inch by 6-inch baking dish; cover with sauce.
Bake, uncovered, at 375° F for about 15 minutes or until fish flakes easily.

Yield: 4 servings; Serving size: 4 oz. fillet with sauce
Each serving provides the following:
 Calories: 177
 Total fat: 4 g.
 Saturated fat: 1 g.
 Cholesterol: 56 mg
 Sodium: 281 mg

ROCKPORT FISH CHOWDER

Low-fat milk and clam juice are the secrets to the lower-fat and saturated-fat content of this satisfying supper soup.

2 Tbsp vegetable oil
1/4 cup coarsely chopped onion
1/2 cup coarsely chopped celery
1 cup sliced carrots
2 cups potatoes, raw, peeled, and cubed
1/4 tsp thyme
1/2 tsp paprika
2 cups bottled clam juice
8 whole peppercorns
1 bay leaf
1 lb fresh or frozen (thawed) cod or haddock fillets, cut into 3/4
   inch cubes
1/4 cup flour
3 cup low-fat (1%) milk
1 Tbsp fresh parsley, chopped

Heat oil in a large saucepan. Add onion and celery and sauté for about
   3 minutes.
Add carrots, potatoes, thyme, paprika, and clam broth. Wrap peppercorns and bay leaves in cheese cloth. Add to pot. Bring to a boil,
   reduce heat, and simmer for 15 minutes. Add fish and simmer for an
   additional 15 minutes, or until fish flakes easily and is opaque.
Remove fish and vegetables; break fish into chunks. Bring broth to a boil
   and continue boiling until volume is reduced to 1 cup. Remove bay
   leaves and peppercorns.
Shake flour and 1/2-cup low-fat (1%) milk in a container with a tight-
   fitting lid until smooth. Add to broth in saucepan with remaining
   milk. Cook over medium heat, stirring constantly, until mixture boils
   and is thickened. Return vegetables and fish chunks to stock and heat
   thoroughly. Serve hot, sprinkled with chopped parsley.

Yield: 8 servings; Serving size: 1 cup
Each serving provides the following:
Calories: 186 • Total fat: 6 g. • Saturated fat: 1 g.
Cholesterol: 34 mg • Sodium: 302 mg

SPINACH-STUFFED SOLE

A scant amount of oil and part-skim mozzarella cheese give this lower-fat dish a Mediterranean flavor.

Nonstick cooking spray, as needed
1 tsp olive oil
1/2 lb fresh mushrooms, sliced
1/2 lb fresh spinach, chopped
1/4 tsp oregano leaves, crushed
1 clove garlic, minced
1 1/2 lb sole fillets or other white fish
2 Tbsp sherry
4 oz part-skim mozzarella cheese, grated

Preheat oven to 400° F.
Spray a 10-inch by 6-inch baking dish with nonstick cooking spray.
Heat oil in a skillet; sauté mushrooms for about 3 minutes or until tender.
Add spinach and continue cooking about 1 minute or until spinach is barely wilted.
Remove from heat; drain liquid into prepared baking dish.
Add oregano and garlic to drained sautéed vegetables; stir to mix ingredients.
Divide vegetable mixture evenly among fillets, placing filling in center of each fillet.
Roll fillet around mixture and place seam-side down in a prepared baking dish.
Sprinkle with sherry and then grated mozzarella cheese.
Bake for 15-20 minutes or until fish flakes easily.
Lift out with a slotted spoon.

Yield: 4 servings; Serving size: 1 fillet roll
Each serving provides the following:
Calories: 262
Total fat: 8 g.
Saturated fat: 4 g.
Cholesterol: 95 mg
Sodium: 312 mg

POULTRY

AUTUMN STUFFED CABBAGE

This hearty entrée uses half ground turkey and half lean ground beef and no added salt for a lower fat and lower salt taste treat.

1 head cabbage	1/8 tsp black pepper
1/2 lb lean ground beef	1 can (16 oz) diced tomatoes
1/2 lb ground turkey	1 small onion, sliced
1 small onion, minced	1 cup water
1 slice stale whole-wheat bread, crumbled	1 medium carrot, sliced
1 Tbsp lemon juice	1 Tbsp lemon juice
1/4 cup water	2 Tbsp brown sugar
	1 Tbsp cornstarch

Rinse and core cabbage. Carefully remove 10 outer leaves, place in a saucepan, and cover with boiling water. Simmer for 5 minutes. Remove and drain cooked cabbage leaves on paper toweling.

Shred 1/2 cup of raw cabbage and set aside.

Brown ground beef, turkey, and minced onion in skillet. Drain fat.

Place cooked and drained meat mixture, bread crumbs, cup of water, and pepper in mixing bowl.

Drain tomatoes, reserving liquid, and add 1/2 cup tomato juice from can to meat mixture. Mix well; then place 1/4 cup filling on each parboiled, drained cabbage leaf. Place folded side down in skillet.

Add tomatoes, sliced onion, water, shredded cabbage, and carrot. Cover and simmer for about 1 hour (or until cabbage is tender), basting occasionally.

Remove cabbage rolls to a serving platter and keep warm.

Mix lemon juice, brown sugar, and cornstarch together in a small bowl. Add to vegetables and liquid in skillet and cook, stirring occasionally, until thickened and clear. Serve over cabbage rolls.

Yield: 5 servings
Serving size: 2 rolls each
Each serving provides the following:
Calories: 257 • Total fat: 9 g. • Saturated fat: 3 g.
Cholesterol: 54 mg • Sodium: 266 mg

CHICKEN RATATOUILLE

Served over rice, this delicious dish is loaded with vegetables and skinless chicken breasts, making it a lower-fat, lower-salt one-dish meal.

1 Tbsp vegetable oil
4 medium-chicken-breast halves, skinned and with fat removed, boned, and cut into 1-inch pieces
2 zucchini, about 7 inches long, unpeeled and thinly sliced
1 small eggplant, peeled and cut into 1-inch cubes
1 medium onion, thinly sliced
1 medium green pepper, cut into 1-inch pieces
1/2 lb fresh mushrooms, sliced
1 can (16 oz.) whole tomatoes, cut up
1 clove garlic, minced
1 1/2 tsp dried basil, crushed
1 Tbsp fresh parsley, minced
black pepper to taste

Heat oil in a large nonstick skillet.
Add chicken and sauté for about 3 minutes, or until lightly browned.
Add zucchini, eggplant, onion, green pepper, and mushrooms.
Cook for about 15 minutes, stirring occasionally.
Add tomatoes, garlic, basil, parsley, and pepper; stir and continue cooking for about 5 minutes, or until chicken is tender.
Broil 6 inches from heat, 15 minutes on each side, brushing with marinade every 5 minutes.
Discard any leftover marinade.

Yield: 4 servings
Serving size: 1 1/2 cups
Each serving provides the following:
    Calories: 266
    Total fat: 8 g.
    Saturated fat: 2 g.
    Cholesterol: 66 mg
    Sodium: 253 mg

Yosemite Chicken Stew and Dumplings

Skinless chicken is the basis of this delicious stew with cornmeal dumplings made with low-fat milk.

For the stew:
1 lb skinless, boneless chicken meat, cut into 1-inch cubes
1/2 cup onion, coarsely chopped
1 medium carrot, peeled and thinly sliced
1 stalk celery, thinly sliced
1/4 tsp salt
black pepper to taste
1 pinch ground cloves
1 bay leaf
3 cups water
1 tsp cornstarch
1 tsp dried basil
1 package (10 oz.) frozen peas

For the cornmeal dumplings:
1 cup yellow cornmeal
3/4 cup sifted all-purpose flour
2 tsp baking powder
1/2 tsp salt
1 cup low-fat (1%) milk
1 Tbsp vegetable oil

For the stew:
Place chicken, onion, carrot, celery, salt, pepper, cloves, bay leaf, and
  water in a large saucepan.
Heat to boiling; cover and reduce heat to simmer. Cook for about 1/2
  hour or until chicken is tender.
Remove chicken and vegetables from broth. Strain broth.
Skim fat from broth; measure and, if necessary, add water to make 3
  cups of liquid.
Mix cornstarch with 1 cup of cooled broth by shaking vigorously in a
  jar with a tight-fitting lid.
Pour into saucepan with remaining broth; cook, stirring constantly,
  until the mixture comes to a boil and is thickened.

Add basil, peas, and reserved vegetables to sauce; stir to combine.

Add chicken and heat slowly to boiling while preparing cornmeal dumplings.

For the dumplings:

Mix together cornmeal, flour, baking powder, and salt into a large mixing bowl.

Mix together milk and oil. Add milk mixture all at once to dry ingredients; stir just enough to moisten the flour and evenly distribute the liquid. Dough will be soft.

Drop by full tablespoons on top of braised meat or stew.
Cover tightly; heat to boiling.

Reduce heat (do not lift cover) to simmering and steam about 20 minutes.

Yield: 6 servings
Serving size: 1 1/4 cup stew with 2 dumplings
Each serving provides the following:
    Calories: 307
    Total fat: 5 g.
    Saturated fat: 1 g.
    Cholesterol: 43 mg
    Sodium: 471 mg

VEGETARIAN DISHES

BLACK BEANS WITH RICE

A delicious Caribbean favorite that is cholesterol-free and made with very little added fat.

1 lb dry black beans
7 cups water
1 medium green pepper, coarsely chopped
1 1/2 cups chopped onion
1 Tbsp vegetable oil
2 bay leaves
1 clove garlic, minced
1/2 tsp salt
1 Tbsp vinegar (or lemon juice)
6 cups rice, cooked in unsalted water
1 jar (4 oz.) sliced pimento, drained
1 lemon, cut into wedges

Pick through beans to remove bad ones. Soak beans overnight in
   cold water. Drain and rinse.
In a large soup pot or Dutch oven, stir together beans, water, green pep-
   per, onion, oil, bay leaves, garlic, and salt. Cover and boil for 1 hour.
Reduce heat and simmer, covered, 3 to 4 hours or until beans are very
   tender. Stir occasionally and add water if needed.
Remove about 1/3 of the beans, mash them, and return then to pot.
   Stir and heat through.
Remove bay leaves and stir in vinegar or lemon juice when ready
   to serve.
Serve over rice. Garnish with sliced pimento and lemon wedges.

Yield: 6 servings; Serving size: 8 oz.
Each serving provides the following:
   Calories: 561
   Total fat: 4 g.
   Saturated fat: 1 g.
   Cholesterol: 0 mg
   Sodium: 193 mg

SUMMER VEGETABLE SPAGHETTI

This lively vegetarian pasta dish contains no added fat or oil, is low in cholesterol, and is good hot or cold.

2 cups small yellow onions, cut in eighths
2 cups chopped, peeled, fresh, ripe tomatoes (about 1 lb)
2 cups thinly sliced yellow and green squash (about 1 lb)
1 1/2 cups cut fresh green beans (about 1/2 lb)
2/3 cups water
2 Tbsp minced fresh parsley
1 clove garlic, minced
1/2 tsp chili powder
1/4 tsp salt
black pepper to taste
1 can (6 oz.) tomato paste
1 lb uncooked spaghetti
1/2 cup grated parmesan cheese

Combine the first 10 ingredients in a large saucepan; cook for
   10 minutes and then stir in tomato paste.
Cover and cook gently, for 15 minutes, stirring occasionally
   until vegetables are tender.
Cook spaghetti in unsalted water according to package directions.
Spoon sauce over drained hot spaghetti and sprinkle parmesan cheese
   over top.

Yield: 9 servings
Serving Size: 1 cup spaghetti and 3/4 cup sauce with vegetables
Each serving provides:
   Calories: 279
   Total fat: 3 g.
   Saturated fat: 1 g.
   Cholesterol: 4 mg
   Sodium: 173 mg

B E E F

BEEF STROGANOFF

Using lean top-round beef, plain low-fat yogurt, and very little added salt makes this a heart-healthy dish.

1 lb lean top-round beef, cubed
2 tsp vegetable oil
3/4 Tbsp finely chopped onion
1 lb sliced mushrooms
1/4 tsp salt
pepper to taste
1/4 tsp nutmeg
1/2 tsp dried basil
1/4 cup white wine
1 cup plain low-fat yogurt
6 cups macaroni, cooked in unsalted water

Cut beef into 1-inch cubes. Heat 1 teaspoon of oil in a nonstick skillet.
 Sauté onion for 2 minutes.
Add beef and sauté for an additional 5 minutes. Turn to brown evenly.
 Remove from pan and keep hot.
Add remaining oil to pan; sauté mushrooms.
Add beef and onions to pan with seasonings.
Add wine, yogurt; gently stir in. Heat, but do not boil.
Serve with macaroni.
 Note: If thickening is desired, use 2 teaspoons cornstarch; calories are
 the same as for flour, but it has double thickening power. These calories
 are not figured into the nutrients per serving.

Yield: 5 servings; Serving size: 6 oz.
Each serving provides the following:
 Calories: 499
 Total fat: 10 g.
 Saturated fat: 3 g.
 Cholesterol: 80 mg
 Sodium: 200 mg

VEGETABLES

ITALIAN VEGETABLE BAKE

This colorful, low-sodium, cholesterol-free vegetable dish is prepared without any added fat.

1 can (28 oz.) whole tomatoes
1 medium onion, sliced
1/2 lb fresh green beans, sliced
1/2 lb fresh okra, cut into 1/2-inch pieces, or
    1/2 10-oz pkg frozen okra
3/4 cup finely chopped green pepper
2 Tbsp lemon juice
1 Tbsp chopped fresh basil or 1 tsp dried basil, crushed
1 1/2 tsp chopped fresh oregano leaves, or
    1/2 tsp dried oregano, crushed
3 medium (7-inch-long) zucchini, cut into 1-inch cubes
1 medium eggplant, pared and cut into 1-inch cubes
2 Tbsp grated parmesan cheese

Drain and coarsely chop tomatoes. Save liquid. Mix together tomatoes
    and reserved liquid, onion, green beans, okra, green pepper, lemon
    juice, and herbs.
Cover and bake at 325° F for 15 minutes.
Mix in zucchini and eggplant and continue baking, covered, 60-70
    more minutes or until vegetables are tender. Stir occasionally.
Sprinkle top with parmesan cheese just before serving.

Yield: 18 servings
Serving size: 1/2 cup
Each serving provides the following:
    Calories: 36
    Total fat: less than 1 g.
    Saturated fat: less than 1 g.
    Cholesterol: less than 1 g.
    Sodium: 86 mg

STUFFED POTATOES

Baked potatoes stuffed with seasoned, low-fat cottage cheese are a lavish low-fat, low- cholesterol, low-sodium treat.

4 medium baking potatoes
3/4 cup low-fat (1%) cottage cheese
1/4 cup low-fat (1%) milk
2 Tbsp soft margarine
1 tsp dill weed
3/4 tsp herb seasoning
4-6 drops hot pepper sauce
2 tsp grated Parmesan cheese

Prick potatoes with fork. Bake at 425° F for 60 minutes or until fork is easily inserted.
Cut potatoes in half lengthwise.
Carefully scoop out potato, leaving about 1/2 inch of pulp inside shell.
Mash pulp in large bowl.
Mix in by hand all the remaining ingredients except the Parmesan cheese.
Spoon mixture into potato shells.
Sprinkle top with 1/4 tsp parmesan cheese.
Place on baking sheet and return to oven.
Bake 15-20 minutes or until tops are golden brown.

Yield: 8 servings
Serving size: 1/2 potato each
Each serving provides the following:
    Calories: 113
    Total fat: 3 g.
    Saturated fat: less than 1 g.
    Cholesterol: 1 mg
    Sodium: 136 mg

PASTA

Parmesan Rice and Pasta Pilaf

After the pasta and onion are sautéed, the oil is drained to minimize the fat content of this interesting pilaf.

2 Tbsp Olive oil
1/2 cup finely broken vermicelli, uncooked
2 Tbsp diced onion
1 cup long-grain white rice, uncooked
1 1/4 cups hot chicken stock
1 1/4 cups hot water
1/4 tsp ground white pepper
1 bay leaf
2 Tbsp grated parmesan cheese

In a large skillet, heat oil. Sauté vermicelli and onion until golden brown, about 2 to 4 minutes, over medium-high heat.
Drain off oil.
Add rice, stock, water, pepper, and bay leaf.
Cover and simmer for 15-20 minutes.
Fluff with fork.
Cover and let stand for 5-20 minutes.
Remove bay leaf.
Sprinkle with cheese and serve immediately.

Yield: 6 servings
Serving size: 2/3 cup each
Each serving provides the following:
Calories: 172
Total fat: 6 g.
Saturated fat: 1 g.
Cholesterol: 4 mg
Sodium: 193 mg

DESSERT

RAINBOW FRUIT SALAD

Good as a side dish or dessert, this salad made from fresh fruit is naturally low in fat, saturated fat, and sodium and is cholesterol-free.

Fruit salad:
  1 large mango, peeled and diced
  2 cups fresh blueberries
  2 bananas, sliced
  2 cups fresh strawberries, halved
  2 cups seedless grapes
  2 nectarines, unpeeled and sliced
  1 kiwi fruit, peeled and sliced

Honey orange sauce:
  1/3 cup unsweetened orange juice
  2 Tbsp lemon juice
  1 1/2 Tbsp honey
  1/4 tsp ground ginger
  a dash of nutmeg

Prepare the fruit.
Combine all the ingredients for the sauce and mix.
Just before serving, pour honey orange sauce over the fruit.

Yield: 12 servings
Serving size: 4 oz. cup
Each serving provides the following:
    Calories: 96
    Total fat: 1 g.
    Saturated fat: less than 1 g.
    Cholesterol: 0 mg
    Sodium: 4 mg

CRUNCHY PUMPKIN PIE

This pie uses only a small amount of oil in the crust and skim milk in the filling to make it heart-healthy.

For the pie crust:
- 1 cup quick-cooking oats
- 1/4 cup whole-wheat flour
- 1/4 cup ground almonds
- 2 Tbsp brown sugar
- 1/4 tsp salt
- 3 Tbsp vegetable oil
- 1 Tbsp water

For the pie filling:
- 1/4 cup packed brown sugar
- 1/2 tsp ground cinnamon
- 1/4 tsp ground nutmeg
- 1/4 tsp salt
- 1 egg, beaten
- 4 tsp vanilla
- 1 cup canned pumpkin
- 2/3 cup evaporated skim milk

Preheat oven to 425° F.

Mix oats, flour, almonds, sugar, and salt together in small mixing bowl.

Blend oil and water together in a measuring cup with a fork or small wire whisk until emulsified.

Add oil mixture to dry ingredients and mix well. If needed, add small amount of water to hold mixture together.

Press into a 9-inch pie pan and bake for 8-10 minutes, or until light brown.

Turn down the oven to 350° F.

Mix sugar, cinnamon, nutmeg, and salt together in a bowl.

Add eggs and vanilla and mix to blend ingredients.

Add pumpkin and milk and stir to combine.

Pour into prepared pie shells.

Bake for 45 minutes at 350° F or until knife inserted near center comes out clean.

Yield: 9 servings; Serving size: 1/9 of a 9-inch pie
Each serving provides the following:
Calories: 177
Total fat: 8 g.
Saturated fat: 1 g.
Cholesterol: 24 mg
Sodium: 153 mg

INDEX

boldface indicates boxed text   underscore indicates chart

italic indicates diagram

D

Don't miss these great books in the groundbreaking How to Fight series:

- *How to Fight Cancer & Win—*
  over 150,000 copies sold
- *How to Fight Prostate Cancer & Win*
- *How to Fight Arthritis & Win*
- *How to Fight Heart Disease & Win*

Dear Loyal Reader,

One of the best things you can do for your health is also one of the simplest; become an informed patient. It may seem almost too simple, but studies show that being more informed can actually lead to shortened hospital stays and less overall fatigue, disability, and health distress. It seems that the more we know about our health and the illnesses that threaten our well being, the better off we are.

We have made it our mission here at Agora Health Books to provide you with the most up-to-date and un-biased health information we can find; information that you can put into action. Only books that meet our most stringent standards are chosen to be included in our **How to Fight & Win** series. As a result you can trust that each book in this unique series is written in an even-handed and easy-to-understand manner, and is packed with actionable advice that you can begin to put to work for you right away.

These all-in-one source books are designed to give you the straight story on mainstream, complementary, and natural approaches to specific illnesses. Unlike some of the other biased books you might have run across in the past, each title in the **How to Fight & Win** series take a balanced and fair look at all the methods of preventing and treating an illness or disease.

You don't need to be a doctor to make decisions about your health. What you do need is to be able to see the bigger picture. With a complete understanding of the illnesses that threaten your well being, and the latest information on the best conventional, and alternative prevention and treatment options, you will finally be in the driver's seat and on the road to good health.

Don't wait any longer to take control and begin making educated health-care choices. Become an active participant in your own health-care decisions. Order your **How to Fight & Win** books now and experience what it is like to feel informed, empowered, and in total control of your health.

To your good health,

Alice E. Jacob

Alice E. Jacob, Managing Editor
Agora Health Books

(Cut along dotted line and return to AHB, P.O. Box 977, Dept. M680HTFS, Frederick, MD 21705-9838)

Order Form

To order any of the books in the **How to Fight Series** simply check the title(s) of the book(s) you want, fill in the number of copies you wish to order, add in the appropriate amount of shipping and handling (see box below), and mail in this completed form.

❑ **How to Fight Cancer & Win** ___ copy/copies at **$19.95** ea. $_____
  [680SFCBK]

❑ **How to Fight Prostate Cancer & Win** ___ copy/copies at **$19.95** ea. $_____
  [680SBPRO]

❑ **How to Fight Arthritis & Win** ___ copy/copies at **$19.95** ea. $_____
  [680SHFA]

❑ **How to Fight Heart Disease & Win** ___ copy/copies at **$19.95** ea. $_____
  [680SFHD]

1-3 books add $5.00 shipping and handling
4-9 books add $10.00 shipping and handling
10+ books add $15.00 shipping and handling

SUBTOTAL: $_____

SHIPPING & HANDLING: $_____
(see S&H box for details)

TOTAL: $_____

Check method of payment: *(All orders processed in US dollars.)*

❑ My check is enclosed for $ _____ made payable to **Agora Health Books**.
  (Maryland residents add 5% sales tax)

❑ Please charge my: ❑ Visa ❑ MasterCard ❑ American Express ❑ Discover
Card #:_____ Expires:_____

Signature:_____

Ship to:

Name:_____

Address:_____

City:_____ State:_____ Zip:_____

Phone: (_____)_____

E-mail: _____
(required to receive FREE health updates)

Mail in your order today!
Agora Health Books • PO Box 977 • Dept. M680HTFS • Frederick, MD 21705-9838

**For fastest service call 1-888-821-3609 and ask for code M680HTFS
or fax your credit card order to 1-410-230-1273**

M680HTFS

PRO-I